We
Need to
Talk

Robert & Rosemary Barnes

WORD PUBLISHING
Dallas•London•Vancouver•Melbourne

Scripture quotations marked NIV are from The Holy Bible, New International Version. Copyright © 1973, 1978, 1984, International Bible Society. Used by permission of Zondervan Bible Publishers.

Scripture quotations marked TLB are from The Living Bible, copyright © 1971. Used by permission of Tyndale House Publishers, Inc., Wheaton, Illinois, 60189. All rights reserved.

Library of Congress Cataloging-in-Publication Data:

Barnes, Robert G., 1947–
    We need to talk : opening doors of comunication with your mate / Robert and Rosemary Barnes.
        p.   cm.
    ISBN 0-8499-3589-X
    1. Communication in marriage.   2. Interpersonal communication.   3. Interpersonal relations.   I. Barnes, Rosemary, 1949– . II. Title.
    HQ734.B2487   1994
    646.7'8—dc20   94–11025
                                                                  CIP

456789 LB 987654321

Printed in the United States of America.

Contents

Part 4
OVERCOMING COMMUNICATION
OBSTACLES BETWEEN SPOUSES

Part 5
HEART-LEVEL COMMUNICATION

Acknowledgments

Thanking all those who helped make it possible for Rosemary and me to write this book is a monumental task. As with our previous books, we remain grateful to Fred and Lyn Hunter for the use of their mountain home. It provided the perfect secluded setting for our whole family to get away while we outlined this book.

The rest of the team at Sheridan House Family Ministries cheerfully picked up much of the slack for us while we completed the book. We are very fortunate to have as staff administrator Bob Geissinger as well as his team of Carol Stewart, Nancy Norling, Pam Gardella, and Duane Siers. Their handling of the arms of the ministry and all the administrative details is a great relief of pressure. The heart of the ministry—Sheridan House for girls and Sheridan House for boys—seems to run better when we are writing and away from the day-to-day activities. We are privileged to have Steve Bodnarchuk and Jeri Southerland respectively at the helms of those two ministries. They made it possible for us to get away.

The well-muscled legs of Sheridan House Family Ministries—each of the children's homes—jog along frighteningly well without our interference. Our gratitude is extended to Jack and Janet Ray, Ed and Ann MacDougall, Gil and Yvonne Gilmore, John and Diane Prechtel, as well as Lisa Trinca, Brian Vann, and Paul Duame—a great team for us to have the privilege of working with.

Don McCulloch, Kevin Groenevelt, and my personal secretary, Lillian Hughes, share the day with me at the counseling center. After each of our office meetings, Rosemary and I are in the habit of digesting their input. There are many who come to the counseling center, telling their stories. Of course, all of

7

protect the privacy of those whose stories we used. Their help was invaluable.

We remain grateful for the vigilance of Nancy Norris at Word. Her friendship and the professional way she kept us on schedule have been a great encouragement.

Last, we both remain amazed at the privilege our Lord has given us, not only to have such great friends, but the opportunity to collect this information and put it into book form. God is certainly gracious!

Introduction

I had just finished a long plane flight and was walking out of the elevator to my hotel room. The lady at the desk had already asked me if I needed help with my luggage. It was late, and I didn't want any more delays, so I replied, "No." She also asked me if I knew how to use their new key system. Again I indicated that I didn't need any help. Actually I just wanted to get to my room and crash.

Arriving at the hotel room door, I opened the hotel visitors folder and found a strange looking plastic "key" that looked more like a baseball card than a key. There was a slot above the door knob, so I inserted the card into it. *How hard could this be*, I wondered. Nothing happened . . . so I pulled the card out and tried it again. When nothing had happened by the third try, I began turning the card around in every conceivable direction.

All I wanted was to get the door open. On the other side of this locked door was a huge, freshly made bed. There was a nice, warm shower. I couldn't see the bed or the shower yet, but I could certainly envision them. They were there . . . I *knew* they were there . . . if only I could get this door open!

Then my worst fear happened! While vigorously jamming this little plastic baseball card into the ridiculous-looking "keyhole," I broke it off! In my frustration to get the door open, I had made matters much worse.

This is often the case with communication in marriage. We often want it so badly that we mistakenly close the doors to communication even tighter in our zeal to open them. The doors to communication may have been open slightly during the dating process, but now they appear to be slammed shut. In fact, the doors to communication now appear to be stuck . . .

stuck because the hinges haven't been oiled properly . . . stuck because the husband and wife never learned how to open them properly.

Today's society offers many ways to communicate. We leave each other little notes on yellow sticky pads that adhere to the refrigerator. We leave each other quick little messages on our answering machines. While these are all forms of communication, marriages need a whole lot more than quick little messages on answering machines and yellow sticky notes. Mountains can be built in marriages when there is too much silence! While *We Need to Talk* is a "how to" book to teach husbands and wives how to get beyond the mountains of silence, it is also a book about reaching a heart level, naked communication. Yes, husbands and wives can reach this level of communication even after the doors to communication have been shut for a long time . . . even if those doors were never really opened at all!

Those marital doors to communication can be opened again! In fact, they must be opened so couples do not miss out on experiencing what their marriage can really be. It is our hope that *We Need to Talk* will serve as a usable "key" to open the doors to increased, enhanced communication. But always remember—no matter what kind of door key is available, it is always the responsibility of the user to take hold of the door knob . . . and turn it. Nobody can do it for you!

May we suggest that the most productive way to use this book is for husbands and wives to read it together, out loud. Stop along the way to consider the questions at the end of each chapter and use the time spent answering them as "oil" for those rusty door hinges! We're all used to being talked to (watching television does that for us). But each of us needs oiling now and then when it comes to responding to each other and discussing important issues.

May God bless you and your spouse as you begin the process of opening the doors to communication in your marriage!

Part 1

HOW DID
THESE DOORS
GET SO STUCK?

1

The Noncommunicating World We Grew Up In

Jack was a captain of industry who prided himself in being able to instantly put his hands on the information he needed. In fact, he employed people to do just that. It was their responsibility to keep him informed of the latest happenings and changes in his field . . . hour by hour. Instant communication!

Going out to lunch with Jack was like being embroiled in a network of high technology. He had a cellular phone in his car and carried another tiny cellular with him when he entered the restaurant. If he somehow missed a call on the car phone, an answering service recorded a message. On top of that, Jack's car also contained a fax machine so he could see all the latest offers on his properties. I found myself almost wishing that some corporate disaster would occur so I could see all these gadgets go into action!

Jack had the ability to communicate in the business world at a moment's notice . . . anytime . . . anywhere. All he had to do was demand . . . and he instantly received the information he needed to make a decision or solve a problem.

As excited as Jack was about all these high-tech forms of communication, I knew that was not why he had asked me to go to lunch with him. Jack and I had nothing in common as far as business was concerned. In fact, I didn't know anything about his line of work. Jack wanted to talk to me about something I excelled in, however; he wanted to talk about his marriage. I discovered that Jack—who used all the best and latest forms of communication in business—could not communicate at home. His communication techniques within his marriage were a disaster.

To Jack, communication meant analyzing something, then fixing it. The person who wanted to communicate with Jack needed to simply state the problem or difficulty at hand . . . then *Jack* would solve it! To him, communicating simply for the sake of getting to know someone better seemed totally unnecessary . . . even foreign. After all, he didn't even know the names of all his employees, let alone know anything about them! And that didn't stop them from working together, did it?

"I don't know what has happened to us at home," Jack began, a little reluctant to even admit there may have been an area of failure in his life. "We don't even seem to know each other anymore. Jane continually told me how lonely she was, so I planned a surprise trip for us to cheer her up. It was a long weekend of skiing with some of the couples that Jane enjoys. I thought it would be good for her to be around people, but it was a disaster." As I listened to Jack detail his marital problems, I suspected that Jane wasn't lonely for people—she was lonely for *relationship*. She returned home from the ski trip even more depressed. It was easy to see that she wasn't looking for fun; she was looking for the door to communication with Jack. But Jack was unable to see that for himself.

This leader in industry was a failure at home because he had no idea how to spend an evening at home just talking with his wife. It amazed me how similar Jack's story was to those of so many other couples I've talked to. Some may not be as successful as Jack in their business conquests, but most were equally baffled by their marital difficulties. They did not know how to communicate at home.

Three hours of sitting on the patio "just talking," as Jack referred to it, was an impossible request. His culture had not prepared him for such a waste of time. His culture had not raised him to relate. Instead, he had been raised to collect information, compete, and conquer. He had not been raised to reveal himself and then listen purely for the sake of better understanding another person. In other words, he had not been taught how to really communicate.

Fact Finders

Today's adult—most especially today's male—is involved in a fact-finding frenzy! We have been taught to digest the daily newspaper as if there could be a pop quiz given on its contents at any minute. On top of that, we find ourselves scheduling our evening around watching the evening news. But if we miss the evening news, we can always watch CNN . . . any time of day. After all, we don't want to be left out in the cold without the latest facts and information on the world's latest happenings!

We don't watch the news in order to think about its contents. We can't possibly process all the news coming our way, so we "employ" editorialists to interpret for us just what all this information means. They may make us furious with their biased and sarcastic commentaries, yet our society is addicted to hearing what they have to say. This must be so, or they would not be paid such exorbitant salaries to do our thinking for us!

That's right—we are no longer a society of thinkers! We have become a nation of collectors of information. When we get "information overload" each week from our weekly news magazines, the paper, and the nightly televised news, we put it all in "park." Rather than taking time to think for ourselves, we do what we saw our parents do. We turn on the television and "veg out" in front of some mindless program that does not require us to process information or use our minds at all.

While writing this book, Rosemary and I spent time at a friend's cabin on Beech Mountain in North Carolina. It's a great place for our family to gather each summer. We have great times together, sitting in front of the fireplace each night, talking for three or four hours before bedtime. These summer trips to Beech Mountain have become times when our family gets to know each other all over again. Why? Because we solve problems? No—because there is no television blaring, there are no urgent projects to complete, and no ringing phone to answer! We just spend time talking and listening to each other.

A friend of ours once asked what we do up there in the mountains. Our youngest son, Robey, replied, "We sit in front of the fireplace, telling stories and talking." The look on our friend's face was priceless. He couldn't understand how anyone could do that! "What could you possibly talk about?" his expression seemed to ask.

Our Grandparents Had No Agenda

For thousands of years our ancestors used communication as their major form of entertainment. When they finished with the dishes each night, they either sat out on the porch if the weather was nice, or they sat in front of the fireplace on colder nights. They had no agenda. They just sat and talked. There was nothing to fix. They did not sit to solve—they sat to relate. As they talked the children gathered around and either interacted or listened. This rich ability to communicate was built into their lifestyles. They did not have to plan for it. It came as a natural end to the daily process. This was no fact-finding end to the day—this was a relationship-oriented end of the day.

Most of us, however, have not grown up in that kind of environment. We did not learn to just sit down to talk. For those of us in this generation, there always had to be a reason—sometimes obvious and sometimes hidden—for communication. Jack was raised as a typical male in this modern culture. He was taught to view everyone as a competitor. He was taught to weigh the words of those around him to see if anyone was trying to take advantage of him or prove that he was not living up to his end of the contract or arrangement. That put a lot of pressure on Jack.

The Little League Syndrome

For many generations the males in our culture—and most recently the females—have grown up in a very competitive, non-friend-oriented environment in which everyone is perceived as a competitor. Girls in middle school might call each other to talk on the phone for thirty minutes about boyfriends and relationships. Boys, however, are very bottom-line-oriented. They just call each other to find out the latest game scores. Everything in a male's world is competition-oriented, and it begins very early.

Competition can be a healthy part of growing up. It can even be fun. But when competition becomes a boy's only form of relationship, his personal growth can be cut off. He does not grow up seeing a friend as someone to share experiences with . . . or to sit by a pond with, just talking and listening. Instead he sees friends as people he would like to compete with. He is constantly measuring himself against his friends, always trying to throw the ball farther or catch the larger fish. Because his friends are all competitors, he misses the opportunity to talk out some of his developing thoughts about life. He is deprived of the practice of opening up.

In addition, we live in a very transient society. Most families move several times during a child's developmental years. This constant moving from one community to the next makes relationships for the average child even more difficult. While he can still join teams and participate socially, he does not develop deep, long-term relationships. It's called the *Little League Syndrome*. The only way today's child knows how to relate is to compete.

Today's child grows up just like Jack, honed and ready to use every conceivable resource in order to win, but inept when it comes to friendship and forming deeper relationships . . . like marriage. How could Jack possibly relate on this deeper level? There had been no time or place or friend to sit with beside the pond, just talking for hours for no special reason. Jack was always too busy developing those competitive skills!

Issue-Oriented Communication

Yesterday's parents afforded a child an additional opportunity for learning communication skills. Take the boy of the past: He grew up on the farm or lived above his family's general store. This child had the opportunity to spend long hours with his mom and dad. The boy raised on the farm walked out to the barn with Dad after dinner, and the boy and his dad spent long hours together, working and talking. They got to know each other. This child grew up seeing that communication simply for the sake of communication was the vehicle by which people are drawn closer together. He did not have to perform at a certain level in order to get his dad's attention. He already had it. So father and son had the opportunity to share many non-performance-oriented hours together.

Many of today's children no longer have that opportunity. Communication between child and parent is typically characterized by necessity only. Only when something needs to be achieved or corrected does today's parent sit the child down to talk, and then the talk is limited to the issue or issues at hand. Thus, communication between parent and child has become issue-oriented. This new parent-child relationship seems more like the relationship between employers and employees. Parent-child communication is no longer for the purpose of furthering the relationship. There is no longer any spontaneous time for that. There are no more evening walks out to the barn. Instead today's parents drop their kids off at gymnastics classes. On the way to gymnastics the conversation that takes place is purely functional: "I'll be back to pick you up in an hour!"

Last Bastion of Talk

The last possible place for family fireside chats to take place used to be around the dinner table. This was the family's common meeting ground—the place where everyone was given the opportunity to share the happenings of his or her day. Families have long since abandoned the dinner hour and the family dinner table. Today's children no longer grow up in homes where the family gathers at the same time to eat. And for those who do, many families invite the "nightly news" to join them so they won't have to talk to each other. Once again the children are the losers in this kind of environment. Today's children miss the lesson of relationship-oriented communication. Consequently they never learn what it means to belong to such a relationship. They never learn to talk simply to further relationships.

Children of Divorce

Jack grew up amid another difficult situation. Like many other children in our society, Jack watched his parents go through a divorce. Not only was there no real communication between Jack's parents, but the things they did say to each other were incendiary. Jack watched helplessly as the two most important people in his world tore each other's hearts out . . . and in the process, tore Jack's heart out too. At a very early age Jack decided that he would never allow anyone to get close enough to him to cause him such pain. While still a child he made the conscious decision to close the door to his heart and throw away the key.

Many children and adults have subconsciously made the same decision. To protect themselves from further pain, they decide to close the door to their hearts and feelings and wedge a chair against the door to make sure it remains closed. In that case, any kind of communication meant to further develop a relationship is too scary for these individuals to handle. In their view, opening that door is just too risky.

The Need to Be Vulnerable

To allow oneself to be so vulnerable seems foolish to the Jacks of this world. To Jack and those like him, it only means that he can be hurt. What it really means, however, is that he will never really find happiness in a relationship. Not sharing to the point of being vulnerable means that Jack will never show another person who he really is. It will take time for Jack to learn to be vulnerable, and it will also take a willingness to risk. This is something that is often difficult for males, and it is certainly difficult for someone like Jack.

In our book, *Rock-Solid Marriage*, Rosemary and I discussed the Sunday school classes we have taught for several years. I think the best illustration of what it means to be vulnerable can be found in relating again the difference between Rosemary's Sunday school class for women between the ages of thirty and thirty-three and the class I teach for men in the same age group.

One Sunday I noticed that Rosemary's ladies emerged from their classroom, wiping tears from their eyes. It occurred to me that this was not an unusual sight. The women were frequently observed dabbing their eyes at the end of their hour-long sessions, while we men would burst out of our classroom, slapping each other on the backs and laughing. Yes, it was quite a contrast.

One Sunday afternoon I asked Rosemary what she did in her class to evoke such displays of emotion. "Nothing," she responded. "We were just sharing special prayer requests with each other." What did she think *we* were doing—sharing bowling scores?

"We have a prayer time too," I responded indignantly. "But we're obviously doing something differently than you. What do you ladies talk about?" I asked.

Rosemary began by relating a list of prayer requests so intimate that I hesitate to share them. "So and so asked us to pray about their marriage because they are having sexual problems," Rosemary revealed. "Another lady asked for prayer as she tries to deal with her post-baby weight." And the list of personal items went on and on. It was apparent that these women were willing to make themselves very vulnerable with each other. Consequently it bonded them together as a Sunday school class.

The men, on the other hand, had a different list of prayer requests. One man asked for prayer for a guy who worked for his uncle back in Iowa—a guy whose name he didn't even know. In fact, the only thing our classmate knew was that the man had been hurt in an accident. Another classmate who worked for the local power company had read in his company newsletter that one of his coworkers—a man he did not know personally—had been injured on the job.

While the ladies were willing and able to become vulnerable, the men were not so willing to share and talk about personal issues. While the women could get close, the men had no idea how to do it. They did not know how to share with friends from their point of need because they had learned to view such sharing as a weakness.

Every Conversation a Challenge To Fix Something

Jack was there to fix whatever problems Jane had. If she wanted to talk to him about something, it must mean that something needed to be fixed. Right? At least that's what Jack thought! So he would listen to his wife for a few minutes and then offer some suggestions . . . ways to *fix* things. Once Jane even said to him, "Jack, would you please just stop! I don't want you to fix this! I just want you to listen!" That totally baffled Jack. Why else would anyone talk about something, if not to fix it? After all, if Jack couldn't find a solution, there probably wasn't one.

The situation between Jack and Jane grew worse and worse. As far as Jack was concerned, failure to find an immediate answer to the issues between him and Jane meant that the problem must be much deeper. Either he wasn't able to fix things after all . . . or the topic under discussion was too ridiculous to even be talking about! It's not hard to imagine which option Jack generally chose. Jane eventually grew tired of always being told that her discussions were ridiculous or that talking simply for the sake of talking was just a waste of time. Before long Jane closed the door to her vulnerability too.

Jack Didn't Know How . . .

By now it must be obvious to the reader that Jack didn't open the door to real communication in his marriage because he didn't know how. That's sad because it made him a very lonely man. There are many "Jacks" in today's culture who are just as lonely. A recent poll stated that the number one reason people come through the doors of a church has nothing to do with their spiritual needs. It has to do with loneliness. People today are lonely and state that they come to church to quench that thirst for companionship.

Our culture has made it difficult for the Jacks of the world to quench that thirst. It's not so bad that they don't know how to relate and communicate—what's worse is that they don't know *why* they need to communicate. Communication is the way one person opens up to make himself known to another person. It's how a person shares his or her feelings. Today's adult, however, is so afraid of feeling that he or she stays busy and avoids any in-depth involvement. That avoidance includes in-depth communication with a spouse. Hence, these individuals find themselves ten years into a marriage and still very lonely. They discover that their loneliness has nothing to do with their proximity to another person. They may sleep next to their spouse and still be very lonely. The loneliness they are experiencing comes from their lack of in-depth, ongoing communication—the kind of communication that means they are willing to open the door to their heart and risk vulnerability.

Jack had been raised and trained to believe that communication at its best was a collection of all the essential facts. That's why conversations with his wife about things they had already discussed usually made him respond with, "You're not going to bring that up again, are you?" His response always upset Jane, and he couldn't figure it out.

I'll never forget a meeting I had with a new staff member at Sheridan House Family Ministries. We had just finished a four-hour staff meeting with all the counselors. As we walked out of the conference room I asked the new guy, Al, if I could buy him lunch. We went out to lunch and Al seemed very tense during the whole meal. As we pulled back into the Sheridan House parking lot after lunch, Al asked, "What was the purpose of our lunch?"

"What do you think?" I asked. He responded cautiously, "I thought I had done something wrong in that marathon staff meeting of yours and you wanted to talk to me about it!"

"The reason for that marathon meeting, as you call it, was so we could all get to know each other a little better," I explained. "But I didn't get to know you any better because you spent the entire time taking notes rather than talking. So I wanted to have lunch with you just because I wanted to get to know you better—

that's all." Al walked away puzzled. I don't think he really believed me. He thought I had a hidden agenda and that I had either found out what I wanted to know or changed my mind.

The primary reason for communication is not to share facts. Fact-sharing is simply the most basic form of communication. Communication at its best is defined as time spent opening the doors to one another's innermost self. Let me emphasize that by restating it: Communication is a long-term process by which two people talk in such a way as to open themselves up to one another and share who they really are.

This would be a tough thing for someone like Jack to do. After all, he knew *what* he was—a captain of industry. But he had no idea *who* he was. He had no idea how he felt about things. He didn't know because he had never taken the time to feel. Did he like who he was? Again he had no idea. He knew nothing more than the fact that he liked what he could accomplish. Take his accomplishments away . . . and Jack was lost.

Marriage could have been an opportunity for Jack to find those things out. Marriage is an opportunity for two people to finally share at a level that will start the process of revealing who they really are. In that sense, marriage is the beginning of real communication.

"Forget that!" was Jack's response. I had just stated that I didn't think Jack really knew how to communicate with his wife. I told Jack that communication was time spent exploring who he was in a safe environment—the company of his spouse. Like a third grader who had just been told he had to hold hands with the enemy—a girl—Jack responded with, "Forget that! That's just too touchy-feely for me. I don't see the need for all that stuff!" His response almost made me laugh, although I knew his marital problems were very serious and very real.

I carefully explained to Jack that marriage allows us to share with someone we aren't competing with. It gives us the opportunity to communicate safely and at the same time get to know ourselves even as we get to know our spouses. It means finally having someone to share ourselves with. But—and this is a big BUT—we must be willing to risk. We must risk going against both our culture and our own self-defense systems. To learn to communicate, we must be willing to risk.

Jack was not willing to risk. He has had two wives since Jane and is still refusing to open the door marked "Communication."

Summary

1. We are a culture of people who like to collect facts—especially current events. We just don't know how to spend time talking about ourselves.

2. Spending time talking is not built into our marriage relationship like it was for our grandparents. We no longer sit on the porch and just talk.

3. Many people today—especially men—view everyone as potential competitors. It's hard to communicate openly with someone we feel competitive toward.

4. In a culture that no longer emphasizes a family time of communication and has produced so many children of divorce, making oneself open and vulnerable does not seem wise.

5. People today are lonely but they don't know how to overcome it. Married partners don't understand the value of opening up with each other.

Communication Keys

1. Name some factors or habits that you believe are hindering in-depth communication in your marriage (work schedule, television, activities outside the home, etc.).

2. Examine one of these communication hindrances. What can be done to get it out of the way?

3. Do you feel that when you and your spouse talk, you actually compete with each other to prove you're right about the things you discuss?

4. When is a good time during the week to talk with your spouse?

2

It Doesn't Fit into Our Lifestyle!

To think that we could possibly set aside three hours a night to talk to each other is ridiculous," Phil told the counselor. "I'd like to sit here and tell you that we'll go home and try, but there's no way we could find a three-hour block of time. That may work for other couples, but we're far too busy for that kind of time commitment."

This couple had come to the marriage counselor in search of help, but they wanted it on their terms. Their marriage was a disaster because they were overcommitted in other areas of their lives. The tragedy was that Phil and his wife really believed they were too busy to set aside three hours a week to talk to each other. They didn't know that they were allowed to drop things from their busy schedules in order to make time together.

It was easy for the counselor to see that this couple didn't have time . . . to be married!

Our Calendars Have Been Stolen

Another couple once asked me in all honesty, "How do you set aside time to talk? Our friends who told us about you said you were going to tell us to set aside a three-hour block of time to read together and share once a week. While we were driving here, we actually got nervous talking about what we were going to say to you if you asked us to do that. How do you pull three hours out of the air?"

As this husband explained their dilemma, I watched both husband and wife and realized they were totally serious. They had no idea that making time to communicate with each other was even possible. "Possible" may not even be the right word. They were actually asking if making time to spend together would be "permissible." Would it be OK to take three hours and just sit somewhere and talk in order to get to know each other all over again?

"Let's take a look at your schedules," I responded. "How do you spend your evenings?"

Your Evenings

"How do you spend your evenings?" is usually a question that causes pride to pop from the chests of many young couples today. These couples are not just sitting around watching television all evening long or reading the daily paper. Many of these couples are involved in some very worthy projects.

As we talked I realized this couple was balancing a lot of activities for their children, church committee work, and other worthy community activities such as the PTA. Theirs was quite a résumé—and it was exhausting them. Worse, it was straining relationships within the whole family.

"Your homework for this next week will be to take a few minutes each night and fill out this form (see the *Communication Keys* at the end of this chapter). Let's document the things you do each evening and weekend so we can look at what can be dropped from your schedule."

The looks on their faces were priceless! This husband looked at me as if I were suggesting that we dispose of a portion of his body. His facial expressions seemed to indicate that he was thinking, "This man didn't really just say *drop*, did he? Surely he meant *rearrange*! We couldn't possibly *drop* anything!"

His wife's face reflected a different response. With her eyebrows gently lifted as if to indicate that she had finally found some sympathy, her features indicated that at last she might receive some permission to slow down and start living. "Could we *really* do that?" she seemed to be asking.

Many times we treat our personal schedules as if we're working for some unseen person whom we've never met. We're not really in charge of "Our Evenings." This fictitious taskmaster just keeps demanding our time, giving us one assignment after another. There is no such thing as turning down one of these assignments! We must say yes to everything that comes our way!

When the principal at our children's school asks us to serve on the Leadership Committee, it's the very least we can do. After all, the education of our children is a very significant endeavor and Rosemary and I want to be a part of the process. Then when the pastor of our church calls to ask us to serve on the Building Committee, we certainly must say yes to that! After all, working for the church is *very* significant!

Our children also have many athletic events in which they need to be involved. Rosemary and I want them to grow into well-rounded adults so we must find time for their involvement in these extracurricular activities. Somewhere in there we must also schedule the necessary time for homework!

Please don't think we are being sarcastic as we write about this subject. Rosemary and I both believe that committees and community activities such as these are extremely important. The problem is we can't do it all. No one can. Perhaps we can *participate* in all these worthwhile events simultaneously, but if we are really honest with ourselves we know that we cannot do a job we'll be proud of because in trying to do everything . . . all at once . . . we are simply spreading ourselves too thin.

Many of us fall into the trap of overcommitment without realizing it. Others just can't say that magic word—"No!" We act as if someone else has sent us out on those all-important evening assignments, speaking to us omnisciently from some far-off mountaintop and ordering us to take on all these tasks.

Ego Driven

"Oh, but that's where you're wrong," James said very proudly. "You asked us to fill out the chart you gave us and we did! I'm serving on all these committees and I have to say that

I am playing a very significant role on each one! Besides that, I'm coaching my daughter's softball team. I'm in there doing what I'm supposed to be doing!"

"And he's proud of it," his wife, Lela, cut in. "He loved filling out your form. It made him proud to see how much he was able to do. James even said one night, 'Look at our chart! I wonder if anyone else we know is able to balance as much.' I think he missed the whole point!"

Lela was right. James was proud of the way he was able to perform in public. He liked the way he was able to fulfill all the requirements of the activities in which he was involved. He had become quite proficient at bouncing between all those meetings. To James' credit, he was just doing what he thought he was supposed to do. He even found himself looking down on people who stayed at home nights. In his view these individuals were not doing their parts to fulfill the needs of their communities.

"James," the counselor began. "You seem to be able to balance quite a lot . . ." James beamed momentarily! "Unfortunately the foundation that is supposed to be holding up your entire balancing act is beginning to cave in! That's where you have failed horribly."

That word "failure" got James' immediate attention. "You seem to be failing at the 'committee work' you need to be doing at home. Correct me if I'm wrong, but you're here with a counselor, spending time out of your busy schedule, because your marriage isn't doing too well. If your marriage caves in, then none of these other outstanding activities will count."

James had heard those words before . . . but he just didn't believe them. He could not fathom the possibility of his marriage falling apart—not until that day in the counselor's office. That afternoon Lela helped him to see that she was desperately hurting over the poor condition of their marriage.

James had spent the first eleven years of their marriage getting his ego pumped up by people outside their home as he served on all those committees. At committee meetings he would hear, "Great job, James!" And those were nice words to hear—

especially when he had no idea how to do anything at home that would win him such plaudits.

It was finally time for James to realize that he was allowed to say "No!" It was time for him to realize that someone else could do a project equally well in his absence. It was time for James to begin to serve on that all-important committee—his home!

PTCM

We are a culture of people who love gadgets. Instead of paper calendars many of us now use electronic pocket calendars. These new gadgets are fun. Some of them have catchy names like "Personal Time Management System," etc.

It's time that we invented a "Personal Time Control Mechanism" to protect our homes! We could call it a PTCM! In fact, our government should make it mandatory for every home to have one because the way we foolishly handle our personal time is nothing short of amazing.

Once when we were on vacation our entire family went to the grocery store together. Our mission? To purchase the food we would need for the week we were to spend at a cabin in the mountains. Without realizing what we were doing we wasted a lot of time pondering the choices on the cereal aisle. There were so many options! We each acted as if it was our personal responsibility to look over every brand.

It's interesting how decisions such as which kind of cereal to buy are made. Our kids were quick to decide. They wanted to choose the one they had seen most frequently advertised on television. They were obviously market-driven. Rosemary wanted to read all the panels on the boxes for nutritional information. As for me, I don't like cereal anyway and it had been a long time since I had even realized how many brands there were to choose from. So I just chose cornflakes.

It struck me, however, that many of us spend more time thinking about what kind of cereal we're going to buy than we do processing our personal time. We know we have the right to choose which cereal we want to buy, yet many of us don't know we have the right to choose how we're going to spend our personal time.

You may decide to play a game of Monopoly this evening as a family. As you set up the board the phone rings. Of course, you answer it. The thought is not, "Should I get this?" but "I hope this call won't take one of us away from the game for too long because this is an activity we have planned to do as a family."

Without even realizing it, we are allowing the caller to determine whether or not our night will be interrupted. The caller chooses a time that is most convenient for him to call us. Whether or not it is convenient for us seems to be irrelevant.

If the caller is a salesperson, we know how to get off the phone in a hurry. If it is a friend, winding up the call may take a little longer. Meantime the family is left playing second place in our personal time management. Their needs have been beaten out of first place by those of a telephone caller.

The same is true for that unexpected knock at the front door. There was a time when a person's home was his sanctuary. Now it's his trap! It's a trap when anyone can have access to a person's home.

Since we no longer protect our families from things that interrupt our time together, whoever rings the doorbell owns a piece of our evening!

Permission to Say No! . . . Please!

Is it rude to say to someone standing at your front door, "Hi, Billy. We're in the middle of doing something important right now as a family. Why don't I have Jimmy call you later?"

No, that's not rude! It's called protecting our family time together. Yes, we need to reach out to those who live around us. But we also need to protect our families from all-out invasion. We live in such mobile times! On one hand, it's a blessing to be able to visit people on the other side of town with an ease that was never imagined in times past. On the other hand, this easy mobility is another reason why our children will spend more time with their peers than with their parents. Unfortunately many families feel they must get away from home on weekends just to be able to spend some time together. It sure seems that there could be a less expensive way!

Rosemary and I suggest that it's time to protect our families and the time we spend together so we can get to know each other again. It means guarding against phone intrusion into the time we have set aside to spend together. Perhaps it even means choosing not to answer the phone during certain hours.

We have discovered one solution to the telephone dilemma. We have invested in a clever and relatively inexpensive little gadget that allows us to screen our calls. It's called an answering machine!

"Oh, I couldn't do that! I couldn't just turn the box on when I'm really at home and *lie* about the fact that I'm there!" There's no need to lie! Why not simply record a message that tells the truth: "You have reached the Barnes residence. We can't come to the phone right now because we are spending time together as a family. Please leave your name and number and we'll be happy to get back with you. Thank you!"

See how easy it is? There's no need to lie. But there is a need to protect. We must accept permission to protect our family time together from the invasion of outside forces. Many of us have grown up unprepared to confront the issue of numerous interruptions and outside invasions. We think we're supposed to accept all those calls and visitors and still have a thriving marriage and family life. But it won't work. Something has to give . . . and most of the time it's the marriage.

It's time to confront that invasion of interruptions! It's time to stop interrupting the things that really count when all is said and done. It's time to decide that a three-hour block of time each week is a goal worth charging toward. As difficult and scary as that may sound, it's necessary in order to protect our marriages, our families, and our futures.

Remember—you are allowed to control your own time schedule. Do it!

Summary

1. Today's couple has lost control of their evenings.
2. Our egos often cause us to say yes to far too many activities that take us away from our families.
3. We need to create our own PTCM (Personal Time Control Mechanism).
4. Give yourself permission to say No!

Communication Keys

Using the "How I Spend My Evenings" form provided at the end of this chapter, take a look at where you and your spouse are really spending your personal time.

Filling out the form will be very time consuming . . . and very revealing. Fill it out carefully, accounting for each fifteen-minute segment of your evening with one of the categories listed below. Total up how many times you list each category. Multiply each total times four (for 4 percent) to find the percentage of your evening that you spent doing each activity. Rosemary and I encourage you to make copies so you and your spouse can each take a look at a whole week's worth of activities.

Question: Are you setting aside enough time to communicate with your spouse?

Categories

Eating dinner—refers to the percentage of time spent eating dinner.

Watching TV—refers to the percentage of time you personally spent watching television that particular evening.

Helping kids—refers to the percentage of time spent helping the children with homework, baths, chores, sports activities, etc.

Chores—refers to the percentage of time you spent on chores around the house (dishes, laundry, mowing the lawn, etc.).

Work—refers to the percentage of time you spent on things brought home from the office or other occupation-related activities.

Communication—refers to the percentage of time spent talking to your spouse without interruptions or without doing anything else simultaneously. Includes time spent in a marital staff meeting.

HOW I SPEND MY EVENINGS

TIME	ACTIVITY	% OF EVENING	TOTALS
5:00		4%	____% Spent eating dinner
5:15		4%	____% Watching TV
5:30		4%	____% Helping kids
5:45		4%	____% Chores
6:00		4%	____% Work
6:15		4%	____% Communication
6:30		4%	____% Other
6:45		4%	
7:00		4%	
7:15		4%	
7:30		4%	
7:45		4%	
8:00		4%	
8:15		4%	
8:30		4%	
8:45		4%	
9:00		4%	
9:15		4%	
9:30		4%	
9:45		4%	
10:00		4%	
10:15		4%	
10:30		4%	
10:45		4%	
11:00		4%	

ACTIVITY #1   Time spent eating dinner
ACTIVITY #2   Time spent watching television
ACTIVITY #3   Time spent helping kids
ACTIVITY #4   Time spent doing household chores
ACTIVITY #5   Time spent on work-related tasks
ACTIVITY #6   Time spent communicating with my spouse
ACTIVITY #7   Time spent doing other activities
                    (community meetings, etc.)

EXAMPLE:

TIME	ACTIVITY	% OF EVENING	TOTALS
5:00	#1	4%	8% Spent eating dinner
5:15	#1	4%	4% Chores
5:30	#4 (Dishes)	4%	4% Work
5:45	#5	4%	

3

Communication:
No Longer Significant?

John and Mary took their communication very seriously. They would strive to meet each day for lunch at the same little restaurant—a quiet, out-of-the-way place where they knew no one would bother them. After all, John and Mary were busy people! A commitment like this did not come easily, but their relationship was a high priority to them so they were willing to work at it.

Some people may wonder what John and Mary found to talk about so intently for an hour or hour and a half each day. Finding topics to talk about was no problem for John and Mary! They had a lot in common and an endless list of things to share with each other.

While the serious approach John and Mary took to communication is admirable, their relationship was not. They were having an extramarital affair.

Why is it that busy people act as if they don't have time to spend working on communication within their marriage? How can some of these same people find the necessary time to have an affair? Those embroiled in extramarital affairs not only manage to find the time to communicate, but they go out of the way to keep the relationship a secret. It would seem that conducting an affair would take up much more time than simply devoting the necessary time to develop communication within the marriage. An affair takes up much more time simply because of the secrecy factor. If that much time was invested in a marriage, it would undoubtedly bear tremendous fruit.

John and Mary saw communicating as a priority. It was significant enough to them that they set a regular time for their communication to take place.

When Rosemary and I were dating we were both incredibly busy. In addition to our college studies we maintained part-time jobs. Along with that we were involved in many extracurricular activities on campus. Somehow with all of these things going on in our lives we found time each day to talk. Communication was important to us.

Why Do People Talk Today?

When was the last time you walked next door to talk to a neighbor? Some of you who read this book maintain very close relationships within your neighborhoods. Most of us today, however, are issue-oriented in our neighborhood communications. We may need to talk to the guy next door about something having to do with our mutual property lines or a neighborhood project. Usually there is a motive to our communication. We need or want something from them, or we might want to inform them about something. Few of us today just walk next door to say, "I'd like to spend an hour just standing around talking so we can get to know each other better."

The way we communicate in today's neighborhood environment pretty much sums up how we relate to our spouses in marriage. "Why do we need to talk so much?" Bill asked his wife. "You would like for us to sit out on the deck and talk for an hour or so each night after the kids are in bed. Talk about what? Why do we need to do that? If you have something you think we need to discuss, just ask me!"

Bill felt that all communication should be issue-oriented. To his way of thinking, if there was a problem or a need, his wife should simply state what the situation was and then they would try to deal with it. Why sit around and do all that *talking* . . . *about nothing?*

Taken to the next step, Bill's logic would be for a busy husband and wife to save even more time by leaving each other "voice mail" messages! Whatever they had to discuss could just be left on each other's "voice mail" and then the other party could respond with the appropriate answer. No, Bill certainly could see no reason to just sit down and talk!

Relationships No Longer Significant

There was a time when a man's word was his bond. Why was that? Because he was part of a society—not just an individual who happened to live in a society. The key words here are "part of" versus "individual." When a person is "part of" a society, group, or family, he must know what others in the group are concerned about. To be "part of" indicates that a person is working toward a better knowledge of those around him.

However, those living in an individual-centered society no longer need to be concerned with those around them as long as their wishes and desires don't infringe on others . . . and vice versa.

When a man's word was his bond there was little need for written contracts. The society he was a part of had taught him to care what others thought of him. His personal name and integrity were important. His integrity was of greater concern than winning or getting the best out of a deal. In his world, relationship rather than victory was his top priority.

In an individual-based society there is very little reason to communicate. As long as the individual gets what he wants, there is really no need for in-depth relationships. As long as his personal rights are intact and his needs are being fulfilled, the individual's priorities are met.

There's that word again—*needs!* That seems to be what our generation has been taught to seek. We have been taught to expect *our* needs to be met! Hence, one's needs must be the key to this generation's communication process. "She's just not meeting *my* needs!" was the answer a man gave when asked why he had decided to come for counseling. He wasn't there to improve his marriage or even to deal with the problems he and his wife were facing. He was only concerned that his needs were not being met. He was being honest.

The Business Arrangement

Why then should we communicate? To be sure that my needs are being understood? Using this standard, today's wedding vows could be amended to " . . . 'til *needs* do us part." We no longer understand the desperate need we have for relationship.

"That's a nice word," an intelligent man once told me. "Relationship, you say? We have a relationship. My wife and I relate to each other. We have divided up the various tasks and responsibilities and we have both committed ourselves to uphold our end of this relationship. That's a relationship. What more is there?"

As I listened to this man's description of what he thought the marriage relationship was supposed to be, I realized that he was very serious about his views. He had no idea what a marriage looked like or what it was supposed to do. He wasn't describing a marriage relationship. He was describing an "arrangement." The individual who takes care of your dry cleaning has the same kind of arrangement. As I continued talking with this friend I stumbled upon an interesting reason why he viewed marriage in this light.

"What was your parents' marriage like?" I asked. "Did they have a similar arrangement?"

"Oh, no! Their marriage was horrible. They never talked. My mother took care of the house and my father took care of paying the bills. They never talked about anything. In fact, I don't think they even liked each other very much. Now that I think about it, they just basically complained about each other and the fact that the other person wasn't holding up his or her end of the bargain. Their 'arrangement,' as you call it, was barely civil. At least with ours, we have an understanding of what we expect from each other and we work hard to make it happen."

I could see that my friend had no idea of what marriage was all about. With that lack of understanding formed during childhood, he simply proceeded with his own marriage utilizing whatever training he had received. He used the training he received in business and the training that observing his parents' marriage had given him to formulate his own views of marriage as an arrangement. To him, marriage was an arrangement of mutuality in which each partner was to meet each other's tangible needs. He viewed marriage as a fifty-fifty relationship. Anything less was just not sound business. Anything less was a contractual violation!

"But He Wasn't That Way Before . . . !"

This man's wife let him talk for a while before she cut in. "You didn't act this way when we were dating! We spent hours sitting on the hill in front of my dorm just talking. Those were the days when you spent time telling me all about your dreams and asking me questions about mine. We used to talk for hours, just for the sake of talking."

There really is a simple answer for a discrepancy like that. This man knew he had to win his mate's affections and in order to do that, he knew he would have to develop their relationship. Though he may not have automatically known how to do that, he decided to work at it. He learned how to date. To win her affections he learned to set aside time for them to talk. He learned how to talk about a whole range of things that his "lady love" would find interesting. He was "making the sale."

After the marriage, however—and after he had "made the sale"—he no longer felt the need to service the account. After all, they were already married!

Was he conscious of his deception? I don't think his was a conscious, devious plot. Was his deception any worse than his soon-to-be-wife making sure that he never saw her in anything but a perfect outfit? She worked hard at doing whatever she needed to do to win his affections. That, too, is somewhat deceptive. After all, that's not the way she will look twenty-four hours a day after the wedding.

They were both simply putting their best foot forward while they were dating. Everyone does that! The problem is that after they were married, this couple's "best foot" became stuck in their "old shoes." They got comfortable and stopped trying so hard. He no longer understood the need to continue trying to communicate. She paid less attention to her appearance when she was at home.

The Biggest Misunderstanding

Perhaps the biggest reason for not seeing the communication process as mandatory within marriage has nothing to do with these things. It is important to note that some people today don't realize that communication is important because they weren't trained that way. It's also important to realize that couples today don't know why they should communicate because the couples they grew up with did not communicate.

Add to that the fact that today's society is a highly competitive rather than cohabitive one. We neither share ourselves nor blend too easily. These are all good reasons why today's married couples fail to see communication as an essential element to their happiness. But none of these reasons is the most significant one.

The biggest reason why the communication process is the "central nervous system" to any marriage can be found when one looks at the very creation of the institution of marriage. *The LORD God said, "It is not good for the man to be alone. I will make a helper suitable for him"* (Gen. 2:18 NIV). Adam had been given certain God-endowed qualities but he needed to relate intimately with another person. Adam was incomplete. If God had wanted Adam to simply have someone to compete with, He would have created another Adam-type being. Instead, God created Eve.

It's interesting to note that God created Eve *from* Adam. It's as if God took Adam apart, created Eve, then said, "Now I want you to work at becoming one flesh again." Because both Adam and Eve were made from one person, they would again have to go through the process of learning to function as if they were one. Two people become one by sharing such an intimacy that their top priority is the other person instead of themselves.

Intimacy like that cannot be achieved without in-depth communication between a husband and a wife. Two cannot become one by only discussing each other's marital job descriptions and topics like who's going to pick up the kids from soccer practice. In-depth communication that leads to marital intimacy necessitates a lifetime of sharing at a very personal level.

"But I've never shared at that level with anyone," Bill blurted out, "let alone my wife!" This poor man had come to view his wife as the adversary! He used the phrase ". . . let alone my wife" as if she were the last one he would want to risk sharing anything intimate with. Why? Because she could inflict pain if she really knew just how vulnerable and insecure he was.

Alone

Why did God do this? Why did He create marriage in the first place? Simply to multiply mankind? No. God could have easily done that without our help or our pleasure in the process.

Perhaps one reason God did things the way He did is that He knew Adam needed to relate intimately to someone else. In so doing, Adam and Eve could become the person he and she was meant to be. Each of us needs the opportunity to relate to another person at a naked, intimate level. Without that, we become lonely. God saw that without Eve, Adam would be lonely. He made the two from one so they could communicate at such an intimate, ongoing level that they would be able to simultaneously meet their own needs as well as the needs of the other.

Communication between a husband and wife must be a priority because it has been a part of God's plan for marriage since the very beginning. But, as is often true with many important things in life, the communication process does not come easily. It takes work. And it takes the realization that communication is very significant.

Summary

1. We have reached a point in our culture where communicating without purpose seems unimportant. Personal relationships are no longer seen as important, as was once the case. Today's relationships must have a utilitarian purpose.

2. Couples take time to communicate when they need to fix something, divide up responsibilities, or get their point across.

3. Couples don't spend much time just talking, like couples of the past used to do. Communicating simply for the purpose of getting to know one another does not take place often in today's society.

4. Today's couples do not know how important the marital communication process is because they didn't see the last generation sitting on the porch talking.

Communication Keys

1. On a rating scale of 1 to 10, how significant do you believe communication in your marriage really is? (Use 10 to rate it as extremely significant and 1 for insignificant.)

2. How do you think your spouse would rate the significance of communication in marriage on a scale of 1 to 10?

3. Where do you think your ideas on the significance (or insignificance) of communication came from?

4. What was your communication like when you and your spouse were dating?

Part 2

WHY PULL OPEN THE DOOR OF COMMUNICATION?

4

It Helps Us Get to Know Each Other

Several years ago when my son Robey and I were cleaning out our garage we made an unusual discovery. Living in South Florida means that we always have a "hurricane pile" on hand. What's a hurricane pile? It's a huge stack of plywood that has been precisely cut to cover our windows in case of hurricanes. We keep our hurricane pile stacked upright in the garage, leaning against one wall. That afternoon when Robey and I moved the plywood to clean behind it, we found a forgotten door that had been long hidden behind the stack of wood.

We knew the door was there—we could see it from the outside of the house. It provided access to our yard from the garage. But because it was obscured from view by a two-foot-thick stack of plywood we just overlooked it. In fact we forgot about it. That door hadn't been used in years.

"Let's see what we can do to open this door, Robey," I said to my son. We took turns trying to push it open, but the door didn't budge. We could see that it would take an incredible amount of work to put the door into operation again, but I was determined to get the door open . . . one way . . . or another. As we went to the workbench to get more tools, Robey asked some very interesting questions.

"Why do you want to open this door, Dad? We've always used the big garage door instead. We've been walking around this door for years. Do we really need to do all this work?"

These were pretty classic questions. Why go to all the effort? Is there really a reason to open a stuck door?

So We Can See What's on the Other Side

That's probably the exact point some couples have reached in their marriages. "This talking stuff is really a big waste of time," one man said. "Why go to all this effort?"

Ray owned a small computer company. Because his company had been experiencing tremendous growth over the past few years Ray had hired several new salespeople. Ray has the same policy about all his new employees: He keeps the interview process going long after they have been hired.

This business owner understands that when he initially interviews a person, he really only gets to know that person's qualifications. Besides that, the interview will probably only tell him what the interviewee wants him to know. He doesn't really get to know who the person is beneath all the credentials until he spends time with that person. So Ray keeps the interview process going long after the person has been hired so he can get to know who he's working with.

Do You Really Know Each Other?

Dating is almost like an interview process. You get to know each other while you're dating but you don't really get to know the other person deep down inside. No one who is in the midst of dating believes that. Everyone who has been married for over a year knows that for a fact.

Marriage changes the relationship dramatically. The initial interviews have all stopped and now the real relationship begins. But this is the most significant time to keep up the interview process. Now more than ever, it's time to find out more and more about each other. What makes your mate tick? What are your mate's dreams?

"I sat there tonight listening to you talk to Tom and Jill, and I was just amazed," Barbara told her husband, Dick. "I thought, 'Who is this person I'm married to?' I've never heard you talk about your dream to someday start a business in North Carolina. Were you just talking . . . or is this something you really think about?"

Dick and Barbara had just spent the evening out having dinner with another couple. For some reason the two couples decided to do something different. Instead of immediately leaving the restaurant after they finished eating, they sat around the table for another couple of hours drinking coffee and talking. It was then that Dick slowly began to share his dream of opening up a small business in another state.

Barbara was shocked to hear her husband share a dream as intimate as this. It sounded wonderful to her, but she never imagined that her husband even thought along these lines. Later she asked, "Why haven't you ever told me about this?" She was both hurt and surprised that something as significant as this had been kept from her. This was certainly not the dream her husband had discussed with her while they were dating. After eight years of marriage Dick had come up with an entirely new vision for their future, and it caught her by surprise.

Most people share dreams and ideas when they date. They do this to see if their dreams mesh with the dreams of the one they are dating. "This is my dream," one partner begins. "Does it match with your dream?" Even if the question is unspoken, it is subconsciously a very real concern and colors and directs conversational topics as both parties probe for common goals and interests. And there are so many dreams . . . dreams about how many children to have, if any . . . dreams about where to live and how to handle careers. All of these are very valuable discussion topics . . . when we are dating.

But discussions like these are even more important to have after the marriage takes place. The dreaming hasn't stopped. Then why is it that so many married couples seem to act as if they no longer need to share their dreams? It's almost as if, now that they are married, there are no more dreams allowed! Just get on the marriage treadmill and don't look around!

Dreamless Marriages Are Destined for Trouble!

Corporations must have think tanks. If they don't, they just keep turning out the same product year after year until they eventually put themselves out of business. It's important to dream about the future.

Couples who stop sharing their dreams are asking for problems. Without dreams, people can feel very trapped. "Is this all I'm going to be doing for the rest of my life? Will I always be trapped on this treadmill with no room to think or dream or change or grow?"

Damaging things can happen to a person who has no dreams. His spouse may become vulnerable to the listening ear of another person outside the marriage relationship. "I don't know how it happened!" Carla moaned as she sat in the counselor's office, crying. "There is a man at work who is very nice. We began talking and slowly we developed a friendship. Over a period of months I began sharing my dreams and aspirations with him like I have never been able to share them with anybody. The next thing I knew, we were in bed."

People have a need to know and be known by another person. That's a basic function of marriage. Marriage is an opportunity to grow into the persons we were always intended to be. Marriage is intended to help create such an atmosphere for personal growth. Too often, however, people believe that their personal growth—not to be confused with professional growth—can stop now that they are married. "Well, this is it: I'm married. I'll buy a house, then I'll buy a bigger one in a few more years, and then it will be time to work on my IRA!"

Marriage is an opportunity to share one's thoughts and dreams with his or her spouse. What will the future hold? How will we grow or change? What are our dreams for the direction our children will take? It's the job of our spouse to listen to us and help pull those dreams out into the open. When a spouse does not fulfill that role of "dream-puller," a coworker or someone else will!

Dreamless marriages also become boring. In these marriages there is nothing left to talk about. Instead of talking, dreamless couples entertain themselves to death. Dreamless boredom is the death of the marriage relationship. In the same way that it would be disastrous for a child's body to stop growing at age ten or eleven, it is dangerous when a marriage stops growing. A child of ten or eleven still has a lot of growing to do. In fact, the growth still ahead of that child will pretty much determine what he or she will look like for the rest of his or her life.

Marriage is the opportunity for a personal growth spurt. The role of communication in marriage is to help couples think through the happenings going on all around them. Lack of communication, on the other hand, is a dream-smotherer. And too much television in lieu of talking is a dream-destroyer.

At the beginning of this chapter, Barbara was beginning to realize that she didn't know who her husband was anymore. Oh, she could still pick him out from a distance and recognize him from behind by the way he walked. But she really didn't know who he was on the inside anymore.

If Dick and several other husbands each wrote a paragraph about what they would most like to do with their lives, then someone typed up their dreams and gave them to Barbara to choose which dream belonged to Dick, she would have been lost. Barbara didn't know what was going on inside her husband.

"Oh, but I ask him what he's thinking about," Barbara said. "He just never seems to want to talk. When he gets home from work he doesn't even want to talk. When the kids are in bed he doesn't want to sit on the porch and talk. He just wants to watch television. When we go to bed he doesn't want to talk. I just figured that he was always tired and there really wasn't much going on inside of him. When I heard how much he had thought through this whole North Carolina plan, it hurt me. It hurt me even more to find out that he had obviously shared his dream in the past with our friend, Tom."

It's Hard to Keep the Interview Going

Barbara learned a lot from this experience. She learned that she didn't know all she would like to know about her husband's life. She also learned that Dick was able to share his heart, but it took the right situation and the right atmosphere. Most importantly, Barbara learned that she couldn't quit trying to communicate with her husband. But she realized that she would have to be more creative.

We tend to keep on growing after marriage. Some couples have stunted their growth because they don't bounce their thoughts off of each other. Other couples grow in directions that are totally independent of one another. To some extent we will all continue to grow. Whether we grow closer together or farther apart is our own decision.

One way to grow together and to keep on getting to know each other is to keep the interview going. Conduct a regular, ongoing diagnostic evaluation of the person you love. As difficult as it may be to get into the thinking processes of your mate, it's mandatory.

The only way to get to know another person is by listening to what he or she says. The key ingredient—listening—will be discussed in more detail in chapter 8. From their night out to dinner with another couple, Barbara learned that when her husband had a listening audience he felt free to share his dreams. She realized that it was this open, no-agenda-type atmosphere that made it possible for Dick to open up. This helped Barbara see things about her husband that she had never known before.

A Diagnostic Listening Tool

I recently took my car to a mechanic for regular servicing. I need my car and wish it could be serviced while I'm driving it. Wouldn't it be nice if some guy could just sit in the passenger seat and work on my car while I'm driving? Then I could keep all my appointments, he could do his job, and everyone would be happy. However, that's not the way it works. A mechanic can't work on my car while I'm driving it around town.

To have my car serviced, I must set a specific appointment to drop off my car and leave it with the mechanic for several hours. My car can be used for nothing else during that period of time. The mechanic hooks a big cord up to something under its hood and a machine tells him how my car is doing. It's pretty amazing. That hi-tech diagnostic test "listens" to my car's entire system—engine, electronics, everything! After a certain period of time, a printout tells the mechanic what—if anything—needs to be done under the hood. The mechanic doesn't reach right under the hood and start working on the engine immediately. He must first perform that diagnostic test. He needs to get to know my car, and his listening device does that for him.

Barbara's diagnostic evaluation of Dick first needed a "garage"—the restaurant. For some, it may be the back patio. A room where the television is blaring is never suitable. Barbara's marriage also needed a diagnostic tool—a listening ear. She needed to listen to Dick and allow him time to develop his thoughts. It would take time.

"Who has that kind of time?" you may ask. How can you afford not to make time? Barbara realized there were several things she didn't know about her husband—things he hadn't shared. It scared her. Whatever it took, she wanted to know her husband as never before. Finding a way to make the communication process work in their marriage was the only way to open new doors into each other's lives.

"Why do you want to open this door, Dad?" Robey asked me the day we found that old hidden door. "We've always used the big garage door instead. We've been walking around that door for years. Do we really need to do all this work?"

Robey had made a good point. We had been taking the long way around, using the big garage door for everything including taking out the garbage. We just got used to going to the trouble of using the big door. Suddenly it seemed like too much effort to force the side door open.

Marriage is like that. Sometimes we get comfortable doing things the hard way. Sometimes we think it's just easier to not try to open the doors of communication after they have been closed for so many years. Yes, it is difficult to pry those doors open, and you must be careful not to do too much damage. But opening them allows a couple to know each other on a level they never dreamed was possible. They will become part of each other's dreams. It's exiting to share the inner dreams of the one you love!

Robey and I finally worked that door open and discovered how nice it was to have easy access to our yard once more. Of course, I must admit that we had left that door closed for so long that to open it, we did quite a bit of damage. Yes, it would have been a lot cheaper to open it years earlier!

Summary

1. When married couples don't communicate, they eventually find out they don't know each other anymore.

2. Everyone has dreams deep down inside, and some people never allow those dreams to surface. It's the job of the marriage relationship to uncover those dreams.

3. Some spouses find they have such a need to share their dreams that they go outside the marriage to find a listening ear. Danger . . . and possible disaster!

4. The communication process allows two people to maintain the lifetime process of getting to know one another. Opening the doors of communication allows a couple to continue getting to know each other in a deeper way.

Communication Keys

1. What are your dreams? List them by the following categories:
   - Personal dreams
   - Dreams for your marriage
   - Dreams for your children
   - Dreams for your future

2. Now do the same for your spouse. Can you list his or her dreams in each category?

3. Take a moment to discuss each other's dreams.

5

Decide Who's Boss

Who elected you to be the boss?" Elaine screamed at her husband, Blake.

"We're not talking about who the boss is here," Blake shouted back. "We're talking about the best way to do this! I'm sick and tired of opening the checkbook and finding the numbers scribbled in third-grader handwriting so that nobody can read it. That's no way to keep a checkbook!"

Elaine was furious! "Third-grader! Is that what I am? Just because I don't happen to agree with you about something, you automatically feel it's your job to take over and try to insult me into agreeing with you. Tuesday you felt like you needed to teach me the proper way to put the silverware into the dishwasher. Who cares! Who cares how the knives and forks go into the dishwasher as long as they get clean! Who wants to be a neurotic like you? Your way isn't the right way—it's just *your* way. You have your way of doing things and I have mine! Who asked you to take charge?"

The argument went on and on about who was right and who was wrong. They had gotten used to this kind of argument. Blake and Elaine thought this battle was about who was supposed to be the boss. They thought that one of them was supposed to win and force the other into doing things their way. They had come to this misunderstanding because they weren't talking.

Marriage Isn't Business

In a business relationship the question of who is boss would have been easily settled by position. The person in the higher

position would have been able to take the coward's way out of
the discussion by saying, "It doesn't matter what you think. I'm
in charge and you'll do it my way—or lose your job!"

A manager might handle his business by dictating ORDERS
without ever listening to the other person's perspective. However,
a good leader certainly would not. We're all different and that
means we all have different ideas. A good leader takes the time to
listen rather than demand. A real leader wants to utilize all the
brain power around him. It's his leadership skills that will bend
others in the right direction for the good of the team.

Taking a Census of Gifts

Eddie was new on the staff at Sheridan House. Fresh out of
school with a master's degree in social work, Eddie was put in
charge of a home for ten teenage boys. That meant he was also
in charge of a set of houseparents. However, the leadership plan
at Sheridan House is not totally hierarchical. Although the
bottom-line responsibility would be Eddie's, he was also responsible to learn to utilize the expertise of the houseparents who had
been working in that home for over a decade. Their experience
meant that in many areas of childcare, these houseparents were
far more knowledgeable than Eddie.

This prospect was very intimidating to our young graduate.
Eddie decided that the best way to begin his new role as super-
visor was to disregard the staff's input into the decision making
process. Instead, he started handing out edicts about how things
were going to be run from now on. He had some good ideas but
not necessarily the best ideas. Whether or not his ideas were
the best was an irrelevant consideration to Eddie. His first order
of business was to prove that he was in charge.

Eddie's approach was a disaster. The key to successful work
in the group home's family setting was for the houseparents
and the counselor to work in unison as a team. Each person on
the team had his or her own gifts and opinions to bring to the
planning meetings. Eddie never took time to listen or even to
discuss anything with the houseparents on his staff. In his

insecurity, he just sent out memorandums dictating how he wanted things done.

The houseparents, with all their expertise in the area of childcare, were being wasted. One brain was being used instead of three. One temperament was being forced upon two other people, and the blending of temperaments necessary for the three to function as a team just never happened. It didn't take long for an explosion to take place.

Everyone Brings His or Her Own Tools

Each person comes into a marriage with his or her own set of "tools" or gifts he or she has spent an entire lifetime learning how to use. Some people are very focused on the task at hand. They care more about getting the job done and getting it done to perfection than they do about the people involved in the process. Other people, however, care more about the relationships around them. They may have a job to accomplish, but if someone needs to talk, they'll stop to talk—even though it means delaying the completion of the task at hand.

That sounds like a perfect blend! If a person who is task-oriented marries a person who is relationship-oriented they can blend together and approach life in a way that will both get the job done and maintain good relationships. They can cover each other's weaknesses while using each other's strengths!

Blake and Elaine went to see a counselor because they could not agree on several issues regarding the training of their children. One night as bedtime was approaching for their daughter, Lindi, Elaine walked into her room and sat down on her bed. She didn't come back out for twenty minutes. By then Blake was furious. Why? Because he felt it was important to teach Lindi punctuality. Eight-thirty was her designated bedtime and Blake was going to see that she met the schedule. He believed that it was important for his daughter to grow up knowing that 8:30 meant 8:30—not somewhere between 8:30 and 9:00.

Blake got Lindi into bed and they said their prayers—all before 8:29. Then Mom walked in . . . while Blake sat downstairs going crazy. He couldn't believe that his wife was causing his daughter to be twenty minutes late! He couldn't believe that Elaine was allowing herself to be manipulated into staying in their little girl's bedroom way past her bedtime!

"How could you do that!" Blake stormed at Elaine as she came downstairs at 8:50.

"How could I do *what?*" Elaine responded in that "What did I do *now?*" tone of voice.

"How could you sit in her room talking so long after her bedtime?" Blake shot back.

"Listen to you," Elaine responded. "My daughter wants to talk to me and you act like it's a crime for me to sit on the side of her bed and listen as she tells me about her day at school. Bedtime is not for the sake of meeting a schedule. It's for our daughter . . . just like talking to her is for her own good. Which is more important—being on time to bed or having an opportunity to talk, uninterrupted, to your parent? Don't answer that! It scares me to think of what you believe is the most important!"

Both parents were right. Together they would do a great job of helping each other to raise Lindi. Blake would help organize Lindi's outside world while Elaine worked to help Lindi organize her emotions and thoughts by giving her time to talk. What a team! But this marriage wasn't a team—it was a disaster! Why? Because Blake and Elaine weren't utilizing each other's best gifts. They weren't even talking.

Mindless Memo Mentality

Couples who don't take time to talk through their differences clobber each other with them! They miss the opportunity to turn those differences into strengths. They miss the opportunity to grow and change and become more well rounded individuals. They miss the chance to become a stronger team. Instead of taking large blocks of time to communicate about their differences and work them out together, they send each other sharp "memos."

In a business environment, people send memos in order to get a fact or an opinion across to someone else. There is no way to respond to a memo. It's just a quick statement . . . a burst of information. We often do the same thing in our marriage: We send out quick, sharp statements.

But remember—we marry opposites. We seem to overlook this dilemma of differences while dating. Then we battle over it after marriage.

We tend to marry people who respond to much of life in a manner that is opposite to the way we respond. If he's a night person, she's a morning person. If he's overly neat, she doesn't care about how the closet looks as long as she can close the door. If she's concerned about being punctual, he doesn't care as long as he eventually gets there.

There is a very good reason why we marry opposites. It rounds off our weaknesses. In areas where Blake is lacking— such as helping Lindi feel loved—Elaine brings a strength. Learning how to organize their lives is very important, but it is not Elaine's strong suit. That's Blake's strength.

Lindi could one day be a very lucky girl. Her parents complement each other by their "opposites." In fact, their puzzle parts fit perfectly. But Lindi will only be fortunate if her parents decide to utilize each other's strengths instead of insulting each other with offensive verbal memos.

Communicate Rather Than Control

A problem always arises when we fail to sit down and talk about the different ways we approach the details of life. Many spouses think it's their job to win. Blake thought it was his responsibility to force his wife to be like him. He truly believed that his way of doing things was the best and only logical way to handle life's problems. It was frustrating for him that Elaine did not see the wisdom of his ways. Didn't she realize how fortunate she was to have the benefit of all his organizational expertise?

That sounds pretty arrogant! But Blake sounds arrogant only because he did not take time to hear why Elaine felt that her approach was just as important as his. Blake was battling for control—not searching for understanding. It got to the point that Blake and Elaine were no longer bothering to listen to each other's point of view at all. What could have been a great team . . . wasn't.

Ask

"What am I supposed to do—ask her why she does things the way she does?" Blake asked the counselor in a very condescending tone. Then he turned to Elaine and asked sarcastically, "Excuse me, Elaine, can you tell me why you purposely allowed Lindi to stay up twenty minutes later than she was supposed to?" Looking back in the direction of the counselor, he continued, "I can't do that—it's stupid!"

At that moment Elaine did the most amazing thing. Instead of being incensed by her husband's insulting attitude, she decided to quietly answer his question. She did not respond to his attitude.

"Blake," she said, getting his attention. He shot around to look at her, expecting a sarcastic response. Then Elaine continued: "You do a great job of helping raise Lindi to be a responsible child. It's your gift. We'd be at a loss if we had to depend on me to teach her how to keep her room clean or get into bed on time. I'm just trying to balance out your gifts by making sure that, with all those necessary rules, Lindi still knows that we love her. I just wanted to sit on the side of her bed and make sure that our daughter has no doubt that her mommy and daddy love her— and that's why we have rules. I'm not trying to battle you for control, Blake. I think we're both in charge here. I'm just trying to do my part—not undo your part."

Blake was totally surprised and melted. Because there was a counselor watching, Elaine had refused to be drawn into a fight. She simply, lovingly, and affirmingly explained why she handled things the way she did. In so doing, she also explained to Blake how her role complemented his role.

It's Good to Hear It, Better to Trust It

Blake actually heard what his wife was saying for the first time. But now he had to go a very significant step further. He needed to accept the fact that her way was a needed complement to his own approach. He had to realize that one way wasn't right and the other wrong. He had to understand that one way was not more important than the other. He had to accept that both his and Elaine's temperaments were necessary for a "teamship" approach to marriage.

Blake had to step out of his comfort zone and trust that it was OK to do things differently than he had always done them. It was going to take maturity to relinquish control. Let's restate that: It takes maturity to accept your spouse's way of doing things . . . to accept your spouse's way of seeing things . . . to adopt your spouse's way of viewing the priorities as your own. In other words it takes a willingness to grow up.

This wasn't true of Blake only—it was equally true of Elaine. They each had to decide to adjust rather than attack. They desperately needed to communicate rather than conquer. They needed to see that they no longer had to fight to determine who would be boss. To make the necessary adjustments, they would have to set aside enough time to learn to understand each other and trust their opinions as complementary.

Time to Listen—Time to Trust

Learning to trust another's way of doing things takes time. One person may believe that the immaculate cleaning of the house means everything . . . while the other person wants four dogs. It takes time to talk, time to trust, then time to thrust yourself out past the narrow walls of the thinking processes that have defined your security.

It's like putting together a puzzle. When our family spends a week each summer at our friend's cabin in North Carolina, we work together as a family on a puzzle. We scatter all the pieces out onto the work area before we begin. Invariably as we begin each puzzle, the task at hand seems insurmountable. It usually takes hours each night just finding the pieces of its outside boundaries. Then after several more nights of long hours the pieces start fitting together more easily. What once seemed like an unworkable mess has finally come together. The night we put the last puzzle piece in place is always very triumphant.

Marriage brings together many differing puzzle pieces. It's not a matter of who's the boss. It's a matter of who's mature enough to blend all those pieces together. And that takes many hours of communication.

Summary

1. Marriages are innately composed of two partners who have opposing gifts. Each spouse has his or her own temperament and different way of doing things.

2. Unfortunately, some spouses believe that it's their job to take charge. They try to be the boss because they believe their way of doing things is the right way and that it is therefore their responsibility to teach the other spouse.

3. If couples don't take time to talk about their differences, they will never have the opportunity to blend into a team.

4. The only way to blend is to talk, listen, and then trust.

Communication Keys

1. What task or function do you and your spouse view from an opposite standpoint (household chores, ways of parenting, etc.)?

2. List each of your views and approaches to these tasks.

3. What steps could each of you take to blend your strengths and weaknesses to benefit your marriage?

6

No More Mind Reading

That's not fair," Danny said to his wife, Doreen. "I asked you what you wanted to do for your birthday and you said, 'I don't care . . . nothing special.' So I took you at your word. Now you tell me two weeks later that you were disappointed that I barely acknowledged your birthday! I asked, didn't I? If you have something you want me to do, just tell me when I ask! I can't read your mind!"

That's the problem. Sometimes wives act as if they want their husbands to read their minds. But husbands can't do that. "Dropped dreams" are often the result of poor communication. She wishes he would be more creative about the way they spend their anniversaries or her birthdays. He wishes she could tell when he wanted to make love. Neither spouse can read the mind of the other—so both their desires and dreams are lost because they don't talk to each other.

Why Doesn't She Tell Me?

"Why doesn't she just tell me what she wants instead of making me guess?" the frustrated husband asked the counselor. His wife cut in with, "There was a time when I didn't have to tell him. He used to be very creative, and that indicated to me how important our relationship was to him. Now he'd rather I just give him a list of what to do so he won't have to spend any time thinking about it."

If this couple had spent the same amount of time talking to each other, she would have revealed to him what her dreams were. She doesn't give him a list of what to do because she wants him to be creative. She doesn't tell him her wishes directly because she wants him to work at their relationship.

But there is another reason. Doreen didn't answer Danny's question about her birthday because she felt that she had already answered it. For months leading up to her birthday Doreen had been showing Danny some of the things she would like to receive as gifts. She had shown him a piece of jewelry in a mail-order catalog and made a comment like, "If you are ever looking for something to get me as a gift, I would love to have these earrings!" She made other comments such as, "It would really mean a lot to me if you bought me a pretty nightgown." Danny didn't think he needed the information at the time, so he didn't pay much attention to it.

When Danny finally asked his wife what she wanted for her birthday—after all the hints she had given him for months and months—she just gave up. "I think Danny would be happier if I would just go out and buy all my own presents," Doreen said in frustration.

And Danny responded, "If that would make you happy, it would be OK with me."

It's a Lack of Understanding

This couple's problem was a lack of understanding. Danny thought it was his job to get his wife the item or items she wanted for her birthday. But that's not what it's all about. It's about the communication process. Doreen didn't want the gift as much as she wanted her husband to make an effort to make her happy. That would have communicated to her that he cared.

If Doreen had simply wanted the end result—the gift—she could have bought it for herself. To demonstrate what she had been feeling, she painted a great word picture for her husband. "Do you remember the golf tournament when you got your first birdie?" she asked her husband.

"Yeah," he responded, "but I really didn't get that birdie." He had fallen right into her story.

"That's right," Doreen agreed. "But it was written on your scorecard as a hole in two—a birdie. The only difference was that at this hole the club pro was teeing off for each tournament contestant. When he hit your ball, all you had to do was go up on the green and tap it into the hole. When I asked you how it felt to get that birdie, you said you felt robbed since you really didn't get it. Even though you got the desired result—a birdie— you didn't get it the way you had dreamed of getting it.

"That's the way I feel when I try to give you hints and you don't listen. Then when it's getting close to the deadline, the day before my birthday—you want me to give you a 'quick list.' I don't want to get my 'birdie' like that either. I feel robbed."

Doreen did a great job of explaining how cheated she felt when she had to tell Danny—word for word—what she wanted for her birthday at the very last minute. She was more concerned about the process than the end result because she wanted to know that Danny had made an effort to get the information about what she wanted as a gift. To Doreen, that was more important than the gift itself.

Both parties were losing because Doreen wanted Danny to be a mind reader and pick up information from her conversations. He wanted a list and she wanted him to be creative. Why was this happening? Because neither party was willing to budge.

I'll Ask If You'll Tell

Although Doreen wished her husband was more creative and spontaneous, she had to decide to help him out. Even though Danny didn't understand what the big deal was about making a special effort to find out what his wife's dreams were, he had to decide to try harder to hear what those dreams were. Both had to decide to help each other.

When you pull into the drive-through of a fast-food restaurant, the employees always know how to keep your order going. "I'll have a double cheeseburger and a Coke," you say.

The person taking your order will then ask you some questions that will help them fill the rest of your order. "Sir, would you like French fries or a hot apple pie with your order?"

Now, everyone knows why these people are asking us these questions—so the restaurant can make more money. That's not what we're trying to do, however, in marriage. But couples can still learn from their technique. These fast-food employees do a good job of drawing more sales from us. They ask us questions. They ask us what we want—so there's no need for mind reading. We know we will only get what we ask for, and until someone asks, we may not realize that we really want a little more than we originally ordered. Sometimes we need to be reminded of what our options are so we aren't disappointed later on.

Out of her frustration, Danny's wife might say that she really doesn't want anything major for her birthday. She may say it's not important that she and Danny do anything special in cele-bration of their anniversary. But Danny needs to take time to complete the order. "Maybe we could take a break tonight after the kids are in bed," Danny might begin. "Then we can talk about what you want for your birthday."

It's a process. Danny wants to find out how he can make Doreen happy. Pleasing her is significant enough to him that he takes time to talk to her about it. Now it's time for Doreen to help him out by telling him what she wants. Even though Doreen may secretly want Danny to "figure it out" on his own, she needs to jump into the communication process.

Many wives spend decades waiting for their husbands to read their minds concerning how they would like to spend their anniversary. Like Doreen, they would love for their husbands to be romantic, creative, spontaneous—but husbands like Danny need help. If Doreen won't talk to him, Danny may never fig-ure out what she wants and both will lose. It's important that he set aside the right amount of time to ask the right questions. It's equally important that she help him win. And to do that, Doreen and Danny need to talk.

Mixed Messages Don't Help

It's bedtime and a husband gives his wife that all-knowing look. To him, the look says, "I hope we're going to make love tonight!" To her, his look says absolutely nothing! After all, she can't read his mind.

In this case the roles are completely reversed from those of Danny and Doreen. This husband wants his wife to know that he wants to make love . . . and he wants her to know it without his saying anything to her. It's as if he wants her to not only be a mind reader but to also be on twenty-four-hour call!

When they go to bed, she rolls over and goes to sleep. Now he's furious! How could she not know what he was thinking? He's given her all the right hints. He even splashed on some cologne after his shower.

Whose fault is it? Once again it's both their faults. She obviously knows he's hinting at something. Yet she chooses to ignore it, hoping it will go away. If she was too exhausted, she could easily have addressed the issue by saying, "I know you want to make love tonight, but I have absolutely no energy left. Could we wait until tomorrow night and then have a great night?" Her husband might still have been disappointed, but at least she explained what was going on with her.

This husband, on the other hand, could have helped the situation by talking to his wife about making love that night. Although it may sound very unromantic, when a couple is having problems communicating sexually, it is very important for them to take time to communicate verbally.

Once again these are the kinds of discussions that need to take place. Forcing another person to be a mind reader and then getting upset over the lack of results wastes time and can be damaging to the relationship.

Enemies to Hearing Each Other's Dreams

Why is it that some people never "hear" the desires of the one they love? There are many enemies that hinder couples from meeting each other's unspoken wants and needs. One of those enemies may simply be the fact that we no longer take time to process what our loved ones are saying to us. There is no "think time" built into our days.

In the past, spouses had think time—time to follow up on all the things their partners had hinted at the night before. Some used the time spent collecting eggs from the henhouse as think time. For others, think time was the time spent doing any routine task that did not require much brain power.

Today we must decide to find our own think time. It may be time spent behind the wheel of a car, driving . . . time spent alone in our car without listening to the radio, tapes, or talking on the cellular phone. During think time we can process what has been said to us and even hinted at by our spouses and loved ones.

It takes both a desire and a decision to think about what a spouse may have said or hinted at. "What is it that she would like me to do?" "How can I make her happy at this particular event or happening?" "What did he really mean when he said those things last night?"

Television is another enemy of the communication process. If we decide to spend more time watching television than we do listening to our spouses and understanding what they say, we have just decided that television is more important than communication. If we decide to spend the time listening and asking questions, we allow ourselves the opportunity to better understand our spouses. Since we are discussing communication and its enemies in this book, we would do well to mention the invasion of television in every chapter!

An additional enemy could be one spouse's unwillingness to give in and let the other partner "win." Though Doreen may not want to tell Danny everything, she should decide that he needs help in this process and talk to him more openly.

When it comes to unmet desires, the spouse who is in need must be willing to initiate a discussion. The other spouse must be willing to sit down and talk, to uncover the problem by asking the right questions. Once again—the communication process takes time . . . and one more ingredient . . .

The Worst Anniversary Ever

When Rosemary and I celebrated our first anniversary we were both in graduate school and that meant we were struggling financially. The next year Rosemary began talking about a friend of hers who had found a good deal at a local hotel. She said her friend had explained that people celebrating an anniversary could get a room for the night at a really great price.

A "find" like that was typical of this friend of ours, whose husband was an accountant. He was always able to hunt out the deals. I didn't say much when Rosemary told me about his latest find because I didn't think much about it.

When our second anniversary rolled around, it was pretty much the same as the first. I personally did not expect a big gift and I really didn't think Rosemary wanted much either, since we were saving for a house. Buying a house was our long-term goal, so that night we exchanged cards, got a bite to eat at an inexpensive restaurant, and went home for the night.

When we got home I could tell something was wrong. Rosemary seemed a little depressed as we walked through the door of our apartment. I had to decide if I wanted to ask her why she was "down." I knew if I asked, it would mean a two-hour discussion. I decided to risk it. I asked.

"You seem a little bit unhappy for someone who is celebrating an anniversary. Did I miss something?"

"Oh, nothing . . . " Rosemary responded. Whatever "nothing" was, it sounded very half-hearted.

Once again I had to make another decision. Should I pursue the questioning, or let her tell me that nothing was wrong even though I knew something was wrong? Deep down inside, I knew that she wanted me to keep right on asking. If she wanted me to keep asking, why then didn't she just tell me what was wrong in the first place? I didn't understand this process. It just didn't make sense.

But whether I understood Rosemary's behavior or not was not the issue. I still needed to pursue my line of questioning until she was relatively sure that I really wanted to know what was bothering her.

"I can tell that something is wrong," I continued. "Obviously I missed doing something or hurt your feelings."

Then Rosemary began to tell me that she had really hoped that we might go to that hotel for the evening. What she had really wanted was for me to surprise her with a special room for the night because, after all, she had left me all those hints! As it turned out, she had actually packed a nightgown in her purse so she would be prepared for my little "surprise."

We missed out on fulfilling each other's dreams because we didn't communicate. Now that she had told me directly how she felt, it was up to me. I suddenly had another decision to make. Should I listen to what she was telling me?

Swallow Your Pride

It was time for me to acknowledge that I really didn't know what Rosemary wanted from me. It was time for me to ask questions. "Rosemary, let's sit out on the porch while you tell me what you think would be your ideal great anniversary."

"I'd feel foolish telling you what I want," she began. "That's not very romantic—me telling you how I want to be treated on our anniversary!"

"Well, then, let me ask you," I responded. "How romantic was it for you to make me guess and end up spending our anniversary splitting a basket of hot wings? Not great, was it! I need you to tell me what you want so you won't ever be disappointed like this again."

At that point she told me in detail how she would like to spend our next anniversary. She included lots of little things— like having me wash the car before we went out and requesting that I wear a tie to the restaurant. These were all things that I could afford to do . . . things I was capable of doing. All these things would have made her feel special, had I taken the time to do them. Now it was up to me to decide whether or not I would swallow my pride.

Why swallow my pride? Because—I'm embarrassed to say—I was so immature that it seemed stupid to me to do all these things simply because Rosemary orchestrated them. The next weekend, however, I found myself washing the car.

Summary

1. In marriages with poor communication, trying to read your partner's mind is very frustrating. Mind reading in marriage occurs when one spouse tries to force the other into guessing what he or she wants instead of stating it openly.

2. It may seem unromantic and unspontaneous to have to explain to your spouse the things you want from him or her, but it certainly saves both parties from disappointment.

3. Make a deal with your spouse that you will ask for input and be willing to receive it when it's given. Sometimes this means swallowing your pride and saying, "All right, it's obvious that I disappointed you this year on our anniversary. How can I do a better job next year?"

Communication Keys

1. What is one area in your marriage where you feel your spouse really doesn't understand what you want?

2. What methods are you using to share your expectations with your spouse? Are you giving hints, or are you willing to set aside discussion time?

3. What are some of the main enemies hindering you and your spouse from obtaining your dreams? How will you deal with these hindrances?

7

It Helps Us Grow Up

One of the most common mistakes newlyweds make is to assume that each is marrying a mature adult. We are really marrying a "maturing" young adult! Whether or not both spouses ever actually become mature adults depends on how much each partner is willing to change and grow. The marriage relationship plays a big role in that growth process.

Life seems to offer two edges to that sword called change. One edge of the sword is called difficulties. When experiencing rough times, a young person has the opportunity to evaluate his or her own life and make the necessary adjustments. Difficulties can force much-needed growth which will shape a young adult into a mature adult. Of course, if that same individual chooses to ignore those opportunities for growth, the difficult circumstances will only make him or her bitter and angry. Going through life's valleys often makes a person take a long look at the direction in which he or she is walking.

Marriage offers the other edge of that sword because the marriage relationship is innately filled with conflict. Whenever there are two individuals living together, striving toward their own personal goals, there is bound to be conflict. Good communication within the marriage, however, offers each partner a sounding board to help him or her grow past the difficulties and conflicts into maturity.

The communication process provides each partner with an opportunity to hear the other's point of view. It helps both partners sort through conflict with the benefit of another perspective. It also offers a chance to be "trained." Training is also necessary in learning to value the other partner's point of view. A person needs to be trained to learn to get along with, then cooperate with, another individual on a daily basis.

We Are Not Trained to Be Marriageable

In past generations there were usually several children in each home. Consequently most children grew up learning how to share. Today's child, however, seems to have acquired some "rights" along the way. Those rights include having his or her own personal toys. This concept is relatively new, since this is perhaps only the second or third generation in which children have had their own personal toys.

Children of the past played with a few toys shared by all the younger members of the family. There were no "G. I. Joes" for each individual child. The children took turns playing with the same toys. In this process they learned to share . . . and they even learned how to negotiate.

Today's child has his or her own toys and he doesn't have to share. Instead he learns very quickly how to use the word, "Mine!" Not only is there no need to negotiate for toys, today's child doesn't even have to share in other areas of entertainment such as watching television. "Honey, if you and your brother can't agree on what to watch on television, then you go upstairs and watch our television."

The ability to share, compromise, and negotiate are all character traits produced by sibling rivalry. These are all necessary skills for adults to have. More significantly, these skills will help an individual grow up and become "marriageable." Unfortunately, these skills are no longer a part of a child's training process. Instead of providing opportunities for siblings to learn to share, compromise, and negotiate, today's parents want to avoid conflict.

Therefore, today's young adults marry each other only to discover that they lack many important relationship skills. Both partners are still very immature. The modern approach is, quite naturally, "I grew up in a home where I had my own things

and all my needs were met. I didn't have to share or compromise. Now I'm married. My spouse is supposed to be here to
meet my needs!" Unfortunately, each spouse believes that the
other spouse is present in the relationship merely to meet his or
her needs. Hence, there is bound to be great conflict.

The Blade of the Tongue

When I was a senior in undergraduate school, I took a
sculpting course as an elective. It was a great opportunity to get
away from my major and learn something new. I recall looking
at a great big glob of clay and the tools I would learn to use,
wondering how I would begin. One of the tools was a sharp,
knife-like instrument.

Mr. Bunzi, the instructor, sat down next to me during the
first class and watched as I took the knife and began to cut away
large pieces of clay. "That tool is not only used to cut things
away," he began. "It can also be used to put portions of the clay
back in the desired locations, as if you were using a trowel."
He took the knife from my hand and began to demonstrate the
technique. "As you can see," he said, "this tool is to be used for
both positive and negative sculpting. It can cut away . . . and
it can also restore."

Likewise, that same principle can be applied to the tongue.
The tongue can be used to "slice" away at other people, leaving
gaping wounds. But it can also be used in the building-up process
created by encouraging words.

As I learned to use my knife in sculpting class, I quickly
discovered that it was much easier to use it to cut away the
clay than to restore it. The process of using it as a trowel to
add clay back to my masterpiece took much more patience,
time, skill, and expertise.

A passage in the Bible—Matthew 12:36—tells us that
we will be held accountable for every word we speak. That's a
sobering thought—especially where the marriage relationship
is concerned.

Fall Out of Old Bad Habits

"It's a waste of my time to try to talk to you," Donna screamed at her husband, Gus. "Every time I ask you for help with a problem I'm having, you just sit there and say something hurtful to me, then go back to watching TV. Why do I even bother coming to you?" Donna was asking her husband to examine a problem she was having with a coworker in her office. In effect she was saying, "Here's my clay. Can you help me sculpt it?"

She wanted to bounce this problem off of her husband in the hope that he might be able to point out something she was missing in this work-related conflict. But Gus didn't want to be bothered. Instead of taking time to talk with his wife, he just wanted to take his "knife" and quickly lop off a big portion of "clay." "You probably said something nasty to her or showed up late for a meeting. You probably did something to make her mad, like you do at home. If you're having a problem with that lady, just ask for a transfer!"

Gus didn't want to be a part of his wife's problem-solving process. He didn't want to help Donna grow by being her sounding board as she processed her problem.

Some time ago I was having a problem with a coworker. Personnel problems are extremely exhausting to me, so on this particular night I was sitting on the back patio, mulling it over in my mind. As I searched for a solution, I decided to talk to Rosemary and benefit from her expertise. Nobody knows me better than Rosemary, and I knew she could easily analyze what was going on. My solution would have been to terminate this person's employment, but before I took such action, I wanted Rosemary's input.

Listen

As we sat together on the patio, Rosemary listened intently as I described the problems I was having with a particular individual. She listened and tried to understand everything she could about the problem I was facing. She didn't interrupt me unless she didn't quite understand what I was saying. Then she only asked pertinent questions. "Has anyone else at work been having problems with this person? Does this person know that you are unhappy with his performance? Does he know that you are considering letting him go? Have you taken time to sit down with this person for an hour and talk through your differences?"

Rosemary was really listening! I could tell by the way she was listening that my problems were important to her. I could easily see that she wanted to help. At the same time, she was helping me to listen to myself. Had I really done the things she asked me about? Had I approached this problem in a mature way?

At first her questions made me mad. Why was she questioning the way I was handling myself? I just wanted her to verify the action I was about to take! I planned to slice this problem person right out of my life. Instead, Rosemary took the knife to me!

She began using the sculpting knife—her tongue—to speak words that helped me grow up in the area of handling other people. She wasn't doing it in a threatening way, even though at first my defensiveness about this issue made me feel like she was attacking me. Finally I realized that she was helping me through a series of very important questions that would determine how I handled the situation. These were questions I may have easily overlooked, and she knew it.

Offer Alternatives

Rosemary utilized her skills as an expert on one very specific area: Me! No other person was in the position to know me and my tactics as well as Rosemary. Living with me all these years, she knows how I sometimes respond when people press my authority. Rather than responding in a mature manner, I usually feel threatened and come back fighting.

Rosemary knew that about me. As she talked with me about the problem, she wanted to make sure I was handling this particular challenge to my authority in a mature manner.

I've already alluded to the difficulty I was having answering her questions. I could have said, "Wait a minute! You sound like *I'm* the one with the problem! Why are you suggesting that I make changes in my approach toward this man?"

I could have responded like that, but it would have gotten me nowhere. I know what Rosemary would have said: "I'm not attacking you, so don't act like I'm your enemy! I'm on your side. I'm just helping you look at all the alternatives."

Offer Opinions

For many couples, marriage is their first opportunity to ask someone for an evaluation. Whether it's a problem or a philosophy of life, there is no one better than a spouse to offer evaluation. One important key is knowing how to cut away at the "clay" without making one's spouse feel threatened. Another key is receiving feedback in a positive, mature manner.

"I might be wrong, so I want you to hear this all the way through," Rosemary began. (I always hate it when she starts out like that! It's a pretty strong indicator that she's about to point out one of my immature areas!) "It sounds like you feel threatened by this guy's popularity with the rest of the staff. No matter what he suggests, you seem to find something wrong with it. You don't treat the rest of the staff like that. In fact, you accept their ideas and help them even when you don't think their ideas are necessarily the best options. Not this guy, however. There's no doubt that he's obnoxious in the way he makes his demands, and he's way out of line in what he did. His actions and attitude certainly make him eligible for termination. But you may want to look at one last possible way of changing the way you handle him."

She gave her opinion and then was silent. She didn't drive the point home. She didn't pound me with it. She had used her knowledge of me to analyze a weakness in my character—insecurity. Then she applied her expertise and wisdom to the problem I was having with this person.

The silence seemed to last forever. I began to get defensive . . . and she let me. She didn't defend her hypothesis.

She just gave me input that I needed for my own personal growth.

A Call for the Question

I wasn't entirely happy with the way this conversation had turned out, but I knew there was some truth to what she said. "What do you think I need to do?" I asked her.

This is perhaps the most significant part of the whole process of marriage partners helping each other grow up. Asking, "What do you think I need to do?" shows that a person really does want to change and grow toward maturity. The partner's response to that question is equally important. Together the couple can work toward finding a plan instead of one spouse just dictating to the other. Times like these are when opposites become very valuable to one another!

People often wonder why God chooses opposites to join in marriage—two people who will spend years trying to become compatible with each other. It's really very obvious. It's so God can use the sculpting knife of each spouse to smooth off each other's rough edges. Opposites can help each other grow and become masterpieces, if they will just allow the process to happen.

Husbands and wives look at the same things so differently! When couples sit down together to plan out a strategy, their opposing approaches will allow both partners to see all the sides to the issues.

"Rosemary, that sounds great, but it's too hypothetical. If I go into this guy's office and say that to him, it just won't work. It will sound too contrived."

Together we can sculpt a workable plan, using our combined skills and our knowledge of one another's strengths and weaknesses.

Given enough time on the patios of life, the communication process can be a great asset to the personal development of couples who are willing to listen.

But What If He Doesn't Ask?

I can hear someone asking now, "But what if my husband doesn't ask the question, 'What do you think I should do?'" At that point a spouse should gently and lovingly bring up the question.

After a discussion like the one that took place between Rosemary and me, the spouse with the problem may not feel secure enough to open up and ask for help. That's when it's the job of the spouse and friend to begin the question for him. "What do you think you're going to do?" Once you've asked, silence should again prevail. Allow the spouse with the problem to decide whether or not he wants to work on a solution. Then ask, "Do you want my thoughts on this situation?"

It's not the solution that's of greatest interest—it's the marital relationship. By taking the risk to talk to each other about life's difficult areas, trust can be built which will allow one spouse to help the other to grow, change, and mature. All these things are accomplished through the communication process.

When communicating to help each other mature, we must be willing to utilize the expertise of the other partner. If one spouse is more organized, the other spouse should be willing to listen when it's time to organize. If one spouse is more relationship-oriented, the other spouse should ask for help in that area.

One evening I became very frustrated with the way my daughter and I were getting along as we worked together on her school project. "Honey, I feel like I'm not getting anywhere with Torrey and her science project," I told Rosemary. "Do I need to be doing something differently?"

"Bob, you're treating her as if she's beneath your intelligence, and that's degrading," Rosemary observed. "Try talking a little more nicely to her and listen to her ideas about how to do the display."

Rosemary knows I can be bossy! Her advice proved very valuable, making it possible for me to get along better with my daughter as we worked together.

A sculptor's knife is a very sharp tool. When we use our tongues to help the ones we love, we must do it in such a way as to leave no scars! Don't offer "advice" that will be painful for your spouse. Decide to work together toward a solution. Refuse to argue or get into battles. If that starts to happen, realize that the knife may have drawn blood and cut too deeply. Use the knife of words only to sculpt in a positive way.

Summary

1. We need our spouses' input to help us complete the maturation process.
2. The communication tool in marriage is a "sculpting knife" to help both spouses look at all the angles of the difficulties they face.
3. Your spouse is the best person to help you analyze your strengths and weaknesses.
4. Don't become defensive when offered feedback by your spouse!

Communication Keys

1. List some areas where you feel your spouse has more experience than you.
2. How can you utilize your spouse's experience in a better way?
3. When your spouse offers input, what are some of the things that he or she says or does that make you defensive?
4. What are some areas where you can be of most assistance to your spouse?

Part 3

DETERMINE TO OPEN THOSE DOORS!

8

Take the Process Seriously

Our family once spent a week at a friend's farm. For a city kid like me, exploring the farm was a great adventure. On one side of my friend's house I discovered an old storm cellar that had been built into the ground. Its door rose up from the ground in an odd slant. It looked like a storm cellar I had seen in the movies. There were those two weathered wooden doors lying there above ground at a forty-five degree angle. I was intrigued. In fact, there was no way I could resist the urge to open those doors and see what a real old storm cellar looked like. Yes, those doors had to be opened!

Without asking for permission or help from my host, I bent over and tugged on one of the doors. I pulled as hard as I could. What I didn't know was that my friend had never tried to open the storm cellar. Pulling for all I was worth, I yanked at the handle . . . but the door didn't budge. All I did was pull my back out. I dropped to the ground in pain. As I was lying there in agony, my friend came around the corner of the house and saw me writhing on the ground. As soon as he had assessed that I would be all right, he broke into peals of laughter.

My friend helped me to my feet. Gently, we walked over to the porch and gingerly, I sat down. Then he said something very interesting—not about the stuck storm-cellar door, but about the art of lifting things.

"One of the first things I had to learn after I made the transition from businessman to farmer was how to lift things," my friend explained. "City people don't do a lot of lifting, so they don't think about it very often. Here on a farm I lift things all the time so I have to make sure I'm lifting the load properly. Otherwise, I can easily find myself out of commission for a few days and lying on the ground, looking like an idiot—like you! Lifting takes preparation. You have to bend down with your legs rather than bending over from the waist. Then you have to stand up, pushing with your legs rather than lifting up with your back. But first you have to make sure that you really can lift the load. There's a procedure to work through, or you could wind up worse off than when you started."

Procedure Setting

My friend was right. Sometimes we just charge right into things without setting the proper procedures ahead of time. There will be times when we are successful in spite of ourselves. There will also be times when failure to think things through and set procedures can lead to disaster.

That theory can also be applied to the communication process. In fact, the whole concept of setting procedures is laced throughout this book. Just in case some of you may have missed it, a strategy for good marital communication should be clearly stated, step by step.

It may sound very elementary or unnecessary to say that a couple must set procedures that will lead them into better communication. Nevertheless, this is true. Organizations that hold regular committee meetings don't wait until some magical moment when all the committee members just run into one another. They set an appointment to meet. They follow procedures to make sure the meeting takes place on schedule so members can communicate. And when a door of communication gets stuck, they decide on the best way to "un-jam" it.

Step One: The Right Time

Everybody has a time of day or day of the week that is more conducive to communication than any other time. As one of those responsible for fundraising at Sheridan House Family Ministries, I have learned that the best time to talk to a potential donor is over lunch. Why? Because that is one time of day when busy people will permit themselves the mental distraction of listening to someone else's visions and dreams.

Proper timing is just as important to the marital communication process. Some people are night owls. They are able to concentrate and talk into the wee hours of the morning. Others are morning people. They can blast out of bed and get an amazing amount of things done before 9:00 A.M. Few people have both of these qualities.

The key axiom of marriage is that for some reason, people usually marry their counterpart. That opposites really do attract is most apparent during these high-productivity times of day. As a rule, morning people marry night people and if that is not understood early in the marriage, it can cause great difficulty. Each spouse will want to talk when he or she is most coherent. Unfortunately, that is generally when the other spouse is incoherent or sound asleep!

Rosemary is one of those rare individuals who happen to be both a night owl and a morning person. Somehow she is able to get up at 5:45 A.M. even after she stayed up reading until 2:00 A.M. However, I am strictly a morning person. Problems arose early in our marriage because Rosemary thought we should go to bed at 11:00 P.M. . . . then begin a lengthy conversation.

Routine person that I am, I start heading for bed at 10:30 P.M. By the time my head finally hits the pillow at 11:00 P.M., it's as if a hypodermic needle pops out of the pillow. Boom—I'm asleep in ten seconds.

Not so for Rosemary. During the first few years of our marriage, she thought that the minute we got into bed we should talk over all those deep things that she'd been saving up all day to share with me. After her opening line or question, she would look over at me and discover that I was sound asleep. She would become very upset and say things like, "How can you already be asleep? I need to talk to you!"

"What do you mean, 'How could I be asleep?'" I would mumble through my first stages of snoring. "Why else are we here in bed?"

Finally it occurred to me that Rosemary and I kept very different time schedules and that we had different definitions of the purpose of going to bed. One night as Rosemary was trying to engage me in deep conversation, I'd had enough. I decided to give her my definition of the purpose of bedtime.

"Rosemary," I began, sitting straight up in bed. "When you think of bedtime, you think it's time to start this lengthy discourse on the events of the day. The problem is, I don't see bedtime in the same way. When I think of the prospects of you and me going to bed together, two possibilities come to mind—and neither one of them happens to be talking!"

She was upset. "When, then?" Rosemary responded. "You don't want to talk when you come home at night . . . so when do you want to talk?"

Rosemary had a good point. I didn't want to talk when I came in the door from work because my brain hadn't caught up to my body yet. Then after dinner, my standard line would be, "I'm just too tired to talk. Let's just vegetate in front of the television." I'm sure that habit started in the earliest years of our marriage, when Rosemary and I were knee-deep in graduate school and working full-time jobs. When we weren't studying, we were vegetating.

Bedtime, then, was Rosemary's last-ditch opportunity to reach me. I didn't realize that we really had no time for communication. We didn't have it because we didn't set it. Like many other couples, I believed that communication should come into our routine spontaneously . . . just sort of happening naturally some evening as we sat around doing nothing. The problem is, we rarely just sat around doing nothing. There was always some important, time-consuming project. Everyone else was getting the best blocks of our time. Our marriage was getting the junk time that was left over—time that nobody wanted or time when we were too tired to concentrate anyway.

It became apparent that Rosemary and I both had a point. Bedtime was not a time when I was capable of communicating with my wife. I wasn't a night person. So we learned to set a specific time for communication. If we hadn't learned to do that, we might never have found the time in the midst of our marriage for anything more than the most mundane talk about things like, "Did you put gas in the car?"

Time to Get Serious about a Calendar

The only way to get the important things done in today's world is to put them on a calendar. We certainly schedule some pretty unimportant things. Along with professional appointments, one may find things scribbled into our calendars like "haircut," "oil change," or "put fertilizer on lawn." One might deem these things important . . . but they're not exactly earth-shattering. Why is it that we feel these activities are necessary enough to add to our calendars but we don't schedule time for our marriages?

We don't schedule time for marriage because we have not been trained to do that. Rarely has anyone told us to put aside weekly time for marital communication. We have not been taught to mark it down in our Day Timers so we don't forget. Chances are, if a person doesn't decide to mark off a block of time in his or her calendar, the communication session won't ever take place.

Relationship-Based Communication vs. Issue-Oriented Communication

When a couple decide to set aside a block of time each week to communicate, they are making a subtle statement. They are saying that their relationship is important enough to set aside enough time to talk together. It's not because something is wrong. On the contrary. This couple want to set aside time to talk so they can develop their relationship more fully and avoid barriers and problems. Couples who don't see to it that they schedule time for communication end up only communicating when arguing.

Larry and Bev were like two ships passing in the night. They rarely talked to each other. She was into the kids and he was into softball. Every now and then they would hit a breaking point—a point where their marriage was so devoid of any loving relationship that they would find little, irritating things about each other to criticize. Then the inevitable explosion would take place.

"Why would I even want to talk to her?" Larry began. "The few times we do talk are disasters! All we do is scream at each other. We seem to be able to point out all of each other's bad points. Then we verbally beat each other up with them! Our marriage isn't much—but it's certainly at its worst when we talk. We *don't* talk—we have a monthly explosion!"

Instead of setting aside time to talk to each other on a regular basis, Larry and Bev waited until they were mad at each other. When one partner started unleashing his or her wrath, the other was also provoked to argue. Regular, scheduled time set aside for marital communication will eventually help a couple like Larry and Bev avoid repeatedly falling into this trap.

Set a Time—the Right Time

It's important to talk to each other about what time is best. Don't just choose a time. Try to choose the best time for both partners.

For Rosemary and me, that proved to be once a week, on Tuesday evening. When the kids were young, it meant getting a baby-sitter. We had tried waiting until the kids were in bed, but by then I was just too tired to be at my best. Those Tuesday evenings were the best investment of time and money that Rosemary and I ever made.

It must be said that this is not an easy thing to begin. When a couple sets that first appointment to communicate, it may seem very awkward. I remember thinking, "What in the world will we talk about for two hours?" It was a little scary. What if we found that we were bored with each other? Fears like those are no reason to avoid this very necessary communication session!

Avoiding the communication process can be very dangerous for a number of reasons. Over the past two decades of marriage counseling, I have heard the same sad story repeated over and over again. "I don't know what happened," a distraught woman would begin. "I guess I was just more lonely than I realized. My husband and I were so busy that we never took time to talk. There was a guy at the office, however, who seemed so nice! Every now and then we would take a break and spend a few minutes talking. It was kind of nice having another person to talk with. He seemed to genuinely care about me, and I found myself actually looking forward to those break times. We became friends through our mutual need to have someone to talk to.

"Then, before I knew it, we were having lunch together. It was all harmless. He was just someone to fill the void. I had nobody to really talk to and this relationship seemed to meet a need. It progressed to the point where we would set a time—just about every day—to meet for lunch. I obviously knew I shouldn't be doing it because I decided that we should meet at the restaurant rather than be seen walking out of the office together. Then one day we didn't come back from lunch . . . because we checked into a hotel."

Busy as she was, she had found a way to set an appointment to talk. The problem was, she didn't set it with her husband. Both she and her husband now wish they had done whatever it took to set those marital communication times—no matter what they had to drop from their lives in order to do it. This wife wasn't looking for an affair. She was seeking to fill an emptiness. She was looking for someone to talk to . . . someone to listen. Now this couple has a long road to walk—trying to find healing for their damaged marriage. But one thing is certain: They now take their weekly communication sessions seriously.

I'll never forget a statement this wife once made when she and her husband were together in the counseling room. "Dr. Barnes, if you ever need someone to come in here and tell a couple how important their weekly time to communicate is, please call me. I wouldn't want any other marriage to go through what ours has been through!"

Need any more be said? Get a calendar of some type and put your marriage in it. Schedule a weekly time for communication with your spouse—a time that's best for both of you.

Step Two: The Right Place

For many years I made the same basic fund-raising mistake. I chose to call on business leaders at their offices. It finally occurred to me that in so doing, I was not getting their full attention. When I tried to discuss Sheridan House with them in their hectic office environment, these businessmen were too easily distracted by phone calls and the mountain of paperwork and memos staring up at them from their desks. Eventually I realized that if I wanted to have a meaningful discussion with them, it would have to be over lunch.

The same principle is true in marriage. I seem to be most sloppy in my communication habits when I am at home. I don't mean to be that way, but it seems that I fall into bad habits when trying to have meaningful discussions at home. There are several reasons. One reason is that home is where I let down my guard and feel like it's OK to be lazy. It's a place where I've learned to relax and it's a place where I can very easily go brain-dead.

Rosemary would say, "Bob, can we just sit and talk tonight instead of getting involved in any tasks? I just need to spend some time running a few thoughts past you." This would be the start of our in-house communication time.

We'd go sit in the den and then I'd get into my special green chair. I don't know what it is about that chair! It's just so comfortable! My whole body seems to instantly become one with that chair. Once I get into it, my brain parks itself and works only minimally from then on. "Are you listening?" Rosemary would ask. And I would respond, "Of course, I'm listening! Now what was that you just said?"

"I know you're not listening! I just told you I was going to buy several new dresses. It was a test to see if we were in the same room! And you said, 'Sure! Whatever you want.' Obviously, you weren't listening," Rosemary accused. "When you say to me, 'Sure, go ahead and spend whatever you want,' I know you didn't hear a word I said!"

The Curse of the Green Chair

Many of us have a comfort zone like my green chair—a place in our lives where we shut down. Once we get there, we disengage. It's not that we don't hear our spouses when they speak. It's just that we are in that special location—a place so comfortable that we hear them but don't listen to what they say.

We don't consciously make the decision not to listen. After all, everybody needs a place where they can put the day in park for a while. "Shouldn't my home be that place of rest?" a man once asked me. "You make it sound like such an effort, Barnes. To listen to you, one would think that more concentration is required when we're at home, in our castles. When do we rest? When do we get a break?"

He didn't see it that way. This gentleman didn't think family relationships should require such effort. He was both right . . . and wrong. Home should offer each of us a place for rest and relaxation. Home is also where we should give our best. Far too often we give our best effort, thoughts, concentration, and planning to our occupations. Then the family—whom we purport to be working for in the first place—gets nothing of us because there is nothing left. We have already spent all of our energies at work.

The "green chair" will get us if we don't think through and plan our family life so we can fit some rest, relaxation, and *communication* into our time at home. Planning must precede everything else! Our best communication with our families does not happen accidentally. Nor does it happen spontaneously in this busy world we live in.

Too Many Undone Tasks

Rosemary and I have often had the privilege of speaking on the topic of communication in the family with many corporate groups. It has always been intriguing for us to see the lengths that various corporations and organizations will go to in order to hold their meetings. Much forethought seems to go into the selection of some of the locations of these meetings.

One such group was holding an annual meeting in Acapulco, Mexico. When we were invited to speak I was ecstatic. I'd never been to Mexico before, let alone an exotic place like Acapulco. During the meeting I asked the CEO of this company why he went to such extremes and expense to take his people to this city. His answer was very interesting.

"I learned this lesson a long time ago while we were still meeting in the large conference center at our headquarters. I noticed that some of these people were coming into the meetings with paperwork. They were ducking in and out of the two-day sessions because they were so close to their desks that they thought they would try to accomplish two things at once. The meetings were important—but they also wanted to get a few other things done.

"In the middle of one of the pivotal sessions, I was standing at the podium up on stage, talking. I glanced down at the other executive leaders on the stage with me only to notice that one of them was organizing his phone message while I was talking. That's when I realized that we needed to hold these meetings far away from our offices. We needed to get away from the day-to-day tasks so we could discuss the more important aspects of this company."

We're like that, aren't we? We're either 100 percent on task . . . or totally in park. At home, we're either trying to accomplish three things at once . . . or we're vegetating! We may be getting all those tasks done, but we may be missing the whole point of why we're here.

Husbands and wives sit at home trying to talk while one spouse reads the paper and the other watches the game on television. He's not really watching the game . . . he's talking to his wife. She's not really reading a magazine . . . she's talking to her husband. It's a routine of distractions. Why do we give our spouses less time than anyone else?

One evening I went so far as to say, "I know tonight's our night to sit on the porch and talk. But why don't we talk while we're hanging the bedroom wallpaper?" It was like saying, "Let's at least accomplish something instead of wasting time communicating!"

It's the same as my trying to talk to a potential Sheridan House donor at his office. He may be hearing me . . . but he's not listening. Instead, he's trying to accomplish two things at once—giving me some time and organizing his desk.

Put the tasks aside. Meet somewhere. Decide to spend your communication time with your spouse as if it is an important meeting. Relaxation will come later. Then relaxation time won't be so tense and uneasy because the really important meeting—marital communication time—will have already been handled.

Can You Be Reached for Comment?

The nice thing about going out to lunch or for a cup of coffee is that you won't be interrupted during your communication time with your spouse. That is, unless you choose to be interrupted!

"I can't believe she destroyed a $500 cellular phone!" Eric stormed, describing his wife's temper tantrum. "We went out to eat, like you suggested. When we got home, all I did was put my phone on the bedside table as we went to bed. When it rang, she went berserk. She destroyed my phone!"

That was Eric's side of the story. His wife's side of the story shed a bit more light on why she had behaved so irrationally. "We went out, all right," Tammy began. "On the way to the restaurant Eric got two calls on his cellular phone. At the restaurant he got three more. In order to receive one of those calls better, he had to get up from the table and go stand somewhere else. Another call came while we were driving home. Then when we were in bed together it rang once more. This time I decided to answer it by

throwing it up against the wall! I don't know why I did it."
Tammy thought for a moment, then added, "Yes, I do! I'm sick
and tired of having to share Eric with anyone who chooses to
call. His business is obviously more important than our relationship. I just wanted to be able to make love with my husband
without wondering if his phone was going to interrupt us."

Then Tammy looked Eric straight in the eye and said, "Eric!
When you're ready to go to dinner with me alone—without
bringing your business—let me know. Until then it's not worth
the pain of wondering what you're thinking about or when we'll
be interrupted again."

One of the greatest things I ever heard while meeting with
a friend in his office was when he called his secretary to say, "No
interruptions, please. Hold all my calls." I felt valuable when he
said that.

When you meet with your spouse for some marital communication time, make sure you choose a place where you can't
be reached for comment. Let the kids or the baby-sitter know
where you are, but tell them not to call unless it's very important.

Rosemary and I have found that it's even important not to
choose a place that's too familiar for our weekly meetings. We
no longer go to that little coffee shop in our neighborhood because we kept running into friends who wanted to talk. They
were interrupting our time together.

When You Must Stay at the Office

There will be times when you can't get out of the house due
to lack of funds or lack of a baby-sitter. That's OK if you are willing to treat your time together seriously. Take the phone off the
hook, or better yet, use an answering machine. Tell the truth.
Tape a message that says you're home but just not accepting calls.

It Takes Some Thinking and Planning

Just as that corporate CEO took time to plan the right location for his company's meetings, married couples need to plan

too. Location and/or privacy may make all the difference in the world where meaningful communication is concerned. It won't happen by accident. Nor will it happen by convenience.

"It all sounds so exhausting, trying to put this together," a man once said to me. "It's just more convenient to sit and talk in our den." He was right. It was more convenient to stay home and talk from his own comfortable "green chair." Unfortunately, it wasn't happening—and that's why he was seeking a counselor's help for his marriage.

Get out of the "green chair"! Decide when and where is best for communication to take place. Set a time to meet and faithfully observe it, and soon the marital communication process will flourish.

Summary

1. Spouses seem to communicate best at opposite times of day. A night-owl spouse is usually married to a morning person, and that can cause communication difficulties.

2. Set a weekly appointment to communicate. Pick a day, time, and place agreeable to both spouses and make that appointment a must!

3. Decide to go to whatever lengths are necessary in order to communicate without interruptions.

Communication Keys

1. What personal time clocks do you and your spouse function on?

2. Set a date to spend a block of time together this week just to talk.

3. What are some possible locations for these weekly meetings?

4. What is your plan to deal with your children so you and your spouse can share some meaningful communication time?

9

"You Must Not Have Small Children!"

This all sounds real nice and neat," a lady said to me in a very sarcastic tone. "How old did you say your children are? I can't imagine where we would ever find time alone to have one of these meetings you're talking about! I guess we'll just have to wait until our children are grown."

She was shocked to find out that our children were the same ages as hers. Her use of the word "find" conjured up the image of small hands constantly pulling at their parents' skirts or trousers for attention. Did she think that time to talk would occur accidentally? No one will "accidentally" find time to talk. Talking to one's spouse is important enough to decide to make time for it.

Without a doubt, parents must come to the decision that setting time to be alone as a couple is mandatory within marriage. Many young parents are so excited about parenthood that they take very poor care of their marriage. These parents feel guilty about spending any time away from their children. They can't quite bring themselves to put their children in the nursery at church, nor can they leave them with a sitter so they can go out for dinner. This mom may be so into the bonding process that she can't even go to the bathroom alone, without her toddlers in tow.

That's very unhealthy. Children should not be permitted to own Mom or Dad. It teaches children about dependability when they discover that a parent will eventually come out of the bathroom or return to the nursery to retrieve them following a church service. Occasional separation of parents and their children actually helps the parent/child relationship. These separations should be graduated into larger blocks of time as the child grows older.

At one extreme are parents who allow their children to smother every waking moment of their time (as well as many of their sleeping hours). At the other extreme are parents who don't read the research. They subcontract out every area of their childrens' lives. It's not a matter of avoiding any kind of separation; it's a matter of dropping the child off at a continual string of alternate caregivers and trainers. Some of these children exist from day care center to gymnastics class to television and then bed.

We must find a balance. Research undoubtedly validates the profound positive impact of spending large blocks of time talking and playing with our children. But parent-child relationships should never be taken to the point that we neglect our marriage relationship.

Seeing parents spend a weekly block of time together, working on their marriage, will provide a great example for the children. It will illustrate to them that their parents view marriage as an extremely significant relationship. It will communicate to them that their parents view marriage as more than simply an arrangement whereby two people work hard to pay the bills, then take turns transporting the kids to sports events. What greater security for children than to know that once a week their parents make time to verify that marriage is the most important relationship on earth? In this age of divorce, a strong marriage will make children far more secure than buying a big, expensive house in the "right" neighborhood.

That's Great—But How . . . ?

Depending on the ages of your children, various plans will need to be to be made to ensure that time can be set aside for your date to communicate with your spouse. Remember—you must create time. First you must ask yourself some questions.

Can you afford to get out of the house for an evening to-gether? Finances play a big role in whether or not you can hold your meeting at a restaurant or coffee shop. Can you afford to go out for a meal or a cup of coffee at a good location that is conducive to talking? Can you afford to hire a baby-sitter? Who can you hire to baby-sit?

I have discovered that baby-sitters can usually be found for parents who plan to do something important. Recently a couple was in my office for counseling. One of their obstacles to setting a date to communicate was the baby-sitter issue, or so they in-dicated. "It's just so hard to be able to afford or find another baby-sitter," the wife stated.

"Oh," I responded. "Have you recently lost a baby-sitter?"

Her answer was very revealing. "No, we have a baby-sitter on Tuesday and Thursday nights when we go to our meetings. As you know, we are involved in network marketing. We've established a regular baby-sitter for those nights. It's just hard to find another sitter so we can go out together."

As soon as the words were out of her mouth, she knew what she had said. Apparently they believed the sales meetings were important enough for a sitter . . . but their marriage was not.

I recommend that couples who are having difficulty finding a baby-sitter contact their local church. A youth minister should be able to recommend a mature young person who is able to baby-sit.

This young mother's response also brought up another issue. Perhaps she was trying to do too much. It was entirely possible that her plate was too full. Perhaps her schedule was too full for the marriage to be squeezed in.

It is important that couples do not permit their lives to get so busy by taking on eight committees at church, softball three nights a week, and a host of other worthy activities. Couples who do that become very out of balance. They become so out of balance that their marriage falls overboard! When establishing a night to hold a marital communication meeting, it is first im-portant to see if anything else needs to be moderated.

Balance is the key! Some may read this chapter and inter-pret it as suggesting that Rosemary and I are advising them to drop out of all church responsibilities. Nothing could be further from the truth. It is important, however, to see to it that couples do not become so busy that there is no time left for marriage.

When a Baby-Sitter Is Not Possible

There are times when a baby-sitter is not an option. There are also ages in the lives of children when a baby-sitter is no longer necessary. When a couple needs to conduct their marriage meetings at home—for whatever reason—it is important to see to it that they have some time to be alone. For those with young ones, that might mean after the children's bedtime. "But I'm so exhausted by then!" one young mother complained. Perhaps that mother should first deal with the issue of exhaustion.

People deal with exhaustion in different ways. Some grab a quick, thirty-minute nap. When our children were toddlers, Rosemary would vanish for thirty minutes or so to take a hot bath. It's important to find a transition period between the end of family responsibilities and the beginning of a marital communication meeting. Whether it is going for a drive, taking a nap, or soaking in the tub, couples must find a way to overcome their exhaustion or the marriage may suffer irreparable damage.

Another way the "no baby-sitter" issue may be handled is to trade off baby-sitting duties with another couple. When our children were very young, we had friends whose children were the same age as ours. We often baby-sat each other's children, taking turns so each couple could benefit from a night out (or in) without the expense of hiring a sitter.

When children are elementary school age, they can be given a task in another room and told, "Mommy and Daddy need some time to talk." Tell them this time is private time just for the two of you. If that is not possible, you must wait until your children are in bed to talk. Instead of watching television, decide to have a marital staff meeting.

"I just find that too hard to do," Lindsey confessed. "What do I say to my kids? Leave us alone right now . . . we have to talk?" Lindsey was a mom who felt she must respond to all her

children's requests. When they were little, she was the mom
who would not even go to the bathroom alone! All her children wanted to go with her.

This young mom needed help to see that she would be an
even better mother if she learned to allow herself some time
alone with her husband. Her kids needed to see that they would
get their share of time with Mom and Dad, but that sometimes
Mom and Dad needed time alone too.

This Dilemma Never Ends

"When our kids were little, I remember thinking that this
would all be over soon," Eddie confided. "As soon as they grew
older, they would be able to be more independent. Then they
got older and they still wanted to be in the same room with us
all evening. In fact, they insisted on being in the den with us so
we had to wait until they were in bed to talk to each other. Then
came the toughest stage. When they became teenagers, they
were able to stay up as late as we did. Then we had absolutely no
time alone together."

This is all the more reason to carve out a special time of
your own to talk. If a couple will do that when their children
are little, the kids will learn that their parents mean business
when they say, "Mom and Dad need to talk. Please don't knock
on our door unless it's an emergency!"

However, you may count on the kids trying to make you
feel guilty! "Oh, you guys are going out again for coffee? That's all
you ever do!" That statement made by one of our children once
devastated Rosemary. She felt so guilty . . . until I pointed
out to her that we had not been out of the house alone together
in three weeks. Think about the importance of what you are
doing and you will realize that what you are doing for your marriage is for the benefit of your children.

"When you stay at home, what do you do—banish them
from the den?" one parent asked in horror.

Rosemary and I have done that! One evening when Rosemary and I were unable to go out for our weekly meeting together,

we decided to spend our time together in the den. Our teenage daughter is used to spending her evenings sitting with us in the den. On this particular night I told her, "Your mom and I need to be alone in the den tonight so we can talk."

Her very predictable response was, "Why can't I be in there?" I responded humorously, "Because Mom and I need time alone, so from 9:30 on you are banished from the downstairs!"

Torrey thought this was hilarious, so she pushed it a little further. "What will happen if I come down into the den?"

I immediately responded with, "You may be embarrassed to find two naked bodies!" Believe me—that was the end of the conversation. Of course, after that Rosemary wasn't sure *she* wanted to spend an evening with me in the den!

That may not be the response you would like to give. It did, however, open a new line of mother/daughter discussions in our home. My daughter needs to know that her parents love each other passionately—no matter how old or "out of it" she might think we are. Though our time together that night was not necessarily meant to be a time of passion, our communication times so frequently seemed to end that way. And in a restaurant over a cup of coffee, that may be difficult! So staying home now and then does have its advantages!

Just Decide to Do It

Parents need time to process all that is going on in their marriage. It's good for their children to see that happening. They need to see their mom and dad taking their marriage relationship very seriously.

If we don't teach our children by example what it means to be married, who will—television personalities?

Yes, children in the home do present some added obstacles when it comes to marital communication. Privacy often seems to be at a premium. Energy may be difficult to come by. But the good news is that these obstacles can be overcome. Even if it means bolting the bedroom door and holding your meetings there, you can find time to communicate.

There is a good rule of thumb regarding whether or not spouses can find time to communicate. If you are able to find time to make love, you are able to find time for a marital staff meeting. If you are not able to find time to make love, go see a marriage counselor *immediately!*

Summary

1. Children can often present obstacles to marital communication.

2. Time must be found, however, for marriage staff meetings.

3. Some meetings can be held away from home by obtaining a baby-sitter. But that is not always possible. Meetings can still be held at home by arranging some private time.

Communication Keys

1. What do you currently do with your children when it comes to finding time for your marital staff meetings?

2. How is it working? Are your children learning that you and your spouse need private time?

3. What additional steps could you and your spouse take to see to it that the children are taken care of during your private time together?

10

The Proper Amount
of Time

The repairman was standing in my garage, look-
ing at my old garage door. It was a beautiful old door but it didn't
work anymore. It required six people to pull it up. Finally the
repairman looked over at me and said, "They don't make doors
like this anymore. It's solid wood and weighs a ton—the kind
that will last forever. I can fix it but it will take a long time—
probably longer than if I just took it out and installed a new
aluminum door. Both will probably cost about the same amount.
It's your decision. What's it worth to you to keep this beautiful
old door?"

Time is valuable. The repairman was honest with me. He
told me he could fix the door but explained that it would take
time. In reality, his time was worth more than the price of a new,
cheaper door.

The value of time is the key to many things in life. Time is
also an important ingredient in the communication procedure-
setting process. It is one of the most difficult areas of decision
making. How much time should a couple set aside for their
weekly communication appointments?

In 1985 Rosemary and I had the opportunity to go to California where we would tape two radio programs with Dr. James
Dobson. We were very excited! Since we were going to be there
anyway, Rosemary and I decided to stay a little longer than just
two days and spend a week driving up the coast of California.

As the time to leave drew closer, I began to get a little nervous about this trip. I wasn't nervous about the radio programs.

I was looking forward to meeting Dr. Dobson. I was nervous about the six days following the programs, when Rosemary and I would be leisurely driving up the California coast.

The plan was that we would spend the week just driving, with no particular destination in mind. We would just drive and talk. Now, how can a person just drive to nowhere? How can there be no goal to attain daily? We had decided that this would be a week of communication. With no goal or destination in mind, would this week feel more like a month? What could we possibly have to talk about for as long as a week?

The first day of our trip was very awkward. We drove a little and talked a little. Then we stopped and shopped. A major portion of the day was spent in silence, broken only occasionally by comments like, "Do you want to stop here and look around?"

As we started out the next day, Rosemary pulled a small devotional from her purse. She began to read aloud. After she finished, we began to discuss the day's devotional reading. The discussion seemed short and exhilarating. I was shocked to realize that we had discussed what that writer had to say for over an hour. It was then that Rosemary and I realized we had found an avenue that would help our communication. Our marital communication from then on was greatly enhanced by reading a daily devotion from that little booklet.

Include a Third Party

Then we decided to try reading another book Rosemary had brought along, called *Talk to Me* by Charlie Shedd (now out of print). She had planned to read it on her own. Instead, we read it together.

"Just a chapter a day," I remember saying. After all, I didn't want to get carried away with this thing! Rosemary read the first chapter. It provoked some good discussion. The next day, however, as she began reading chapter 2, the author seemed to be describing our marriage! I had to say, "Stop for a minute! Is that me? Is he describing me? Is that the way I treat you when you want to talk to me about something?"

This was the most significant day of our marriage up to that point. By bringing in a "third party"—the book, *Talk to Me*— Rosemary and I found it was suddenly possible to talk about our marriage. If not for the help provided in the book, we wouldn't have known where to begin. The book provided a key that unlocked the doors of communication. An even greater key was that we followed up each insight with discussion.

An Hour Alone Seems Scary

"How will we do this?" the husband of eight years began. "I hear you saying that we need to go out to dinner alone, but we haven't really done that since before we got married. Ever since our wedding, we always go out to dinner with another couple. I can't imagine going out, just the two of us—unless, of course, I brought my *Sports Illustrated!*" He was only kidding about bringing along the magazine . . . well, maybe only half-kidding! He just couldn't imagine setting aside such a large block of time for him and his wife to be alone for no purpose other than to talk.

They spent time alone to be entertained. They watched television together. They spent time alone when they made love. But spending time alone to talk was new . . . and very threatening.

It was not just spending time alone that seemed threatening. It was the amount of time. The problem with communicating for short amounts of time is that no one really gets to develop what he or she wants to say. In fifteen-minute conversations, people get defensive rather than allowing the other person to take his or her time to develop ideas.

Spending short amounts of time in communication only encourages one partner to take control of the process. Invariably in these shorter sessions the more verbally adept of the two quickly takes the lead and says what he or she has to say. This leaves the other partner out of time and feeling very frustrated.

The Eternal Staff Meeting

A friend once asked me to sit in on his weekly staff meeting. On Thursday mornings the staff of a large church gathered with all the ministers to talk for two hours before going out to lunch. As I walked into the meeting one of the staffers remarked, "Welcome to America's eternal staff meeting." I didn't know what he meant until the meeting got going. It seemed to last forever. At this meeting, many topics were discussed and many decisions were made concerning the ministry. Before the two hours were up, one of the staff members who hadn't said much up to this point jumped in with a comment. "I think we made that plan for the summer program rather hastily." Everyone looked at him and wondered where he'd been for the last two hours. That decision had been reached twenty minutes earlier!

The senior pastor asked him to elaborate, which he did for about five minutes. When he finished his critique, some of the staffers appeared to feel threatened. Some were very silent. It was obvious that the newer staff members didn't know that it was all right to disagree. The senior pastor asked the staffer a few questions and after a period of discussion, it became apparent that they had made a mistake in their summer plans. Indeed, they did need to rethink the whole thing. I saw the process as both interesting and relationship-enhancing.

Some People Need More Time

I drove to lunch that day with the senior pastor, who asked me, "Did you think that was an 'eternal staff meeting,' as Jack referred to it?"

"At first I thought it was kind of long—almost unnecessarily so—until Alan piped in with his comment about the summer program." Then the pastor and I discussed his philosophy of staff meetings. This pastor didn't want to just sit there once a week and hand down edicts. He wanted to utilize the collective brain power of his staff. He quickly discovered that it couldn't be done in thirty minutes. Some staffers gave quick "knee-jerk" responses, but the thoughts and ideas of some of the others took a little longer to process. The pastor had learned that their input was worth the wait.

It Takes Time to Disagree Agreeably

It doesn't take any extra time to disagree. Anyone who has been married for more than an hour knows that. It takes time, however, to disagree agreeably. If you are able to express your thoughts on an area of disagreement, allow time afterward so you and your mate can talk through each of your opinions on the subject. As you do this, a valuable process will take place.

When each spouse is given the necessary time to process and express his or her opinions, everyone feels safer and more secure. It's important for both partners to know that the marriage relationship does not pivot on whether or not they agree or express the same opinions. That safe atmosphere during disagreements will not develop during short discussions.

It Takes Time to Help Each Other Think

Time spent in a safe atmosphere will allow a couple to think things through rather than simply to react. If a couple sets aside time to talk but spends it attacking each other's opinions instead, the time is wasted. Too much time will be spent trying to launch a counterattack instead of focusing in on the issues at hand.

Time spent at a restaurant or in a quiet place conducive to discussions will afford each spouse the opportunity to think things through and share his or her thoughts. Attitude is a very important part of this process. If a spouse feels threatened or attacked for a differing opinion, the time spent talking will be agonizing. Everyone has his or her own opinion about family matters. Each should be allowed to express opinions without being attacked for opposing views. Each spouse should decide ahead of time to maintain a loving attitude—no matter what the other person's opinion is. In so doing, two brains can be utilized instead of just one.

Take Time to Disagree Agreeably . . . and
Grow Closer

I observed one other thing as I attend the staff meeting of this ministry team. I saw it again when we were having lunch. These individuals actually *liked* each other! I could easily see that they felt secure in their relationships with one another. Why? Because they had each been given an opportunity to put their thoughts out on the table. More importantly, they saw that when they did so, they were not judged for having their own opinions.

Because these staff members realized they could disagree and still be part of the team, they loved the team even more. That's a key ingredient in marriage! If we can have permission to disagree and still love each other, we can grow closer in unconditional love.

"Billy," Linda cried in the counselor's office. "I feel you don't like me unless I agree with everything you say! I love you no matter what your opinion is, but I don't sense that you feel the same way. Everything is fine with us as long as I don't disagree with anything you say!"

Billy wasn't loving his wife—he was trying to bend her. He didn't feel there was any need to set aside time for long discussions. If everyone would just agree with him, everything would be OK. Relationships were caving in all around him . . . and Billy couldn't understand why.

Time Is Crucial

The privilege of discussing something without fear of judgment is crucial. Taking the *time* to do it is even more crucial. "Quickie" discussions rarely allow for differing opinions. Usually one person will be forced to dominate for the sake of expediency. When one person dominates, the marriage relationship is damaged. The other person feels unloved and unvalued. Worse yet, it leaves the marriage limping along on one cylinder. It's out of balance.

Take time to communicate. At first it may seem awkward to talk things over, but why not start with a two-hour cup of coffee at a quiet restaurant? If communication is still difficult, use this book as a "third party" and read it together, discussing its contents and using the *Communication Keys* at the end of each chapter.

One wife in the counseling room said in front of her husband, "It's not even what we talk about that matters when we set aside a specific amount of time for communication. If he would just take the time to talk, it would mean everything to me. If Robert would acknowledge that our marriage is important enough to schedule a two-hour block of time for communication, it would mean more to me than two dozen roses!"

It's like what the repair man said to me when he looked at my old garage door. "What's it worth?" What's your marriage worth? My friend, Louis, put it this way: "If I'd only done all these things two years ago when she was screaming at me to give her time . . . Now she's gone and it's too late."

Summary

1. Good discussions can't take place in fifteen minutes.
2. It takes time for most people to calm down long enough to think and process information during discussions.
3. In large blocks of time set aside for communication, couples can feel secure enough to disagree agreeably.

Communication Keys

1. Do you allow enough time for your spouse to express his or her opinions and ideas during your marital discussions?
2. Do you feel threatened when your spouse disagrees with your opinions?
3. What are some of the topics that you feel most threatened about when talking to your spouse?

11

We All Travel at Different Speeds

One afternoon I came home early and as I walked into the house through the kitchen, I found my wife and one of her friends seated at the table, dabbing their eyes. They had been crying. I excused myself and went right to our study.

Thirty minutes later, after her friend had left, Rosemary came into the study. "What were you two so emotional about?" I asked her. She told me that her friend had received some distressing news earlier that day. "How long had Diane been here when I got home?" I asked. Rosemary's answer shocked me. "She had just arrived a few minutes before you walked in!"

How do they do it? How could these two ladies sit down together and immediately get into such a deep level of communication? Some people can sit for hours with a friend and never communicate so intimately. Yes, we are all certainly different when it comes to the amount of time it takes for us to communicate at deeper levels. Men and women, in particular, are different. Why? Because, like Rosemary and Diane, women can communicate very quickly on a deeper level. That's really amazing to men like me!

We All Communicate at Various Levels

We must understand that there are several levels to the communication process. Some researchers have been able to enumerate more than three levels, but for the sake of examining the marital communication process we will use just three.

Level One: The Grunt Level

The most basic level of communication can be referred to as the Grunt Level. Grunt-Level communication refers to the times of human interaction when we are obligated to say something or respond to someone in a way that requires only the most minimal input. Our answer need not even make sense.

If you are operating on the Grunt Level, you may walk past someone and say, "Hi! How are you doing?" You have just asked a question at Grunt Level! (How are you doing *what?* What does *that* mean?) Furthermore, does your question even indicate that you would like a response? If the person you have just addressed responds, it will probably be with another Grunt-Level remark: "Fine—how 'bout you?" Then you have the green light to respond with "Great! Good to see you!" (Grunt!)

Imagine if someone were to pass me on the street and stop long enough to say, "Hi, Bob! How are you doing?" What if I responded with, "Oh, I'm near suicidal!" The person would probably keep right on walking and grunting, "Great! Good to see you! Bye!" Why? Because that person was grunting—not thinking about anything I just said.

This kind of communication is a trained social interaction. No one really listens to anyone else—unless, of course, there is no response to that initial "How are you doing?" As long as there is a response—any kind of response—everyone keeps right on going about his or her business.

The Grunt Level is hard to break. It's also important to know that there are places, times, and circumstances when the Grunt Level—and only the Grunt Level—will save the day. Take elevators, for instance. Somewhere in the fine print of the plaque on the wall of most elevators—right under the maximum number of people permitted to ride at one time—must be a statement of elevator etiquette in which talking is not permitted. On elevators, anything more than a Grunt-Level nod is unacceptable!

Think about it. An elevator is the smallest room you will ever be closed up in . . . with the most amount of people—

people with whom you have no communication. An elevator is a stage of communication! Each elevator door should have a sign posted on it that reads, "You are now entering a Grunt-Level Zone!"

One day several years ago my brother, Steve, got on an elevator with me as we headed up to a restaurant on the twenty-seventh floor of an office building. Steve, a very creative guy, turned to me and said, "Watch this!" The elevator had been steadily filling up with people and I knew I was in trouble!

Steve broke the first sacred rule of elevator etiquette and turned around to face the other passengers. Everyone knows that eye contact is not allowed on elevators! But Steve made eye contact with everyone. Then he began talking to the passengers. I couldn't believe it! Neither could anyone else. Didn't this brother of mine know that people weren't supposed to carry on meaningful conversations in elevators?

"Did you ever notice that nobody ever talks to anyone when they're on an elevator?" Steve asked the group. "What if this were the place where you were destined to meet your future wife or husband . . . but you didn't talk because you didn't think you were allowed to?"

That was all the other passengers could take. Now Steve was actually asking the group for an intelligent response! I know many of the passengers were just headed up to the twenty-seventh floor to have lunch like we were—but not in the same elevator. One person actually reached over while we were in mid-transit and pushed a button so he could get off on a lower-level floor. He had decided that he would rather wait for the next elevator than to spend another minute in the same elevator with my brother, who had violated the "grunt rule."

We do the same thing at home. Without realizing it, we do it with our children. The kids come in from school and a parent immediately says, "How was school today?" The child responds, "Fine." The parent then asks the next question: "What did you do?" "Nothing," the child answers, parroting the same answer he's given for years. Nothing? A whole day at school . . . and nothing was accomplished? Surely we can't be listening if we'll allow an answer like that! That's no answer—that's an obligatory grunt!

A husband and wife converge at the end of the day. It's six o'clock and she wants to engage in a meaningful conversation. "How was your day, Honey?" she begins. She really wants to know! Perhaps she is aware that he had a very difficult appointment to deal with that day, so she asks: "How did the meeting go?"

She really wants to talk at a meaningful level! He, on the other hand, just grunts a response: "Fine. It went fine." His agenda for communication is to grunt and go no further. Her agenda is to actually begin the evening's relationship. But she wants to talk and find out how he spent his day. He just wants to get home and put it in park for a while, so he grunts an obligatory response. He doesn't want to talk right now. Grunt!

Level Two: The Journalist

The second level of communication—the Journalist Level—is very similar to the way a journalist responds to life. He or she reports the facts, then gives an opinion about them. This level is significantly deeper than Grunt Level. By talking on the Journalist Level, people get to know what their spouses think. On this level, people express their ideas and their judgments. They give their opinions about the world around them and topics like politics, finance, other people, etc. But notice that these are strictly opinions. Their real feelings about these things are not expressed.

The American male has been trained to operate on this level. On the Journalist Level, communication is quick and easy. Life can be neatly handled with a few short sentences.

Mary and Fred were sitting in the counselor's office. She complained to the counselor that they never talked. "That's not true, Mary!" Fred responded, sounding very surprised. "Why would you say that we don't talk? When you want to sit down and talk about something, I'm always willing. Take the other night, for instance. You wanted me to come away from the television set and talk to you about what we were going to get the kids for Christmas. Didn't I do just that? The problem is that you want to talk about it forever! You want to run it into the ground!"

Mary and Fred were both right. They talked to each other . . . but they talked on different levels. Fred thought Mary wanted to know the logistics of what they were going to be able buy the kids for Christmas. How much could they spend? When should these items be purchased? Fred's opinions on the topic only required about ten minutes to present.

But Mary didn't want his opinions—she wanted to talk to him about it at length. The whole thought was foreign to him. He was legitimately confused when she kept saying, "I didn't want you to give me the facts! I wanted to talk with you about it. I wanted to sit there and think together about the children's Christmas list."

The problem is that most men are no longer taught to do much more than report the facts, then give an opinion. The facts are important, but there is also a need to go further. It is important to be able to talk now and then about how all those facts "taste." How do we feel about the situations we are involved in?

Journalists just report the facts, then give a little editorial about them. It's very hard for the journalist to go much deeper on short notice. This is the man who knows that Grunt Level will never do when his wife asks about his day. At the Journalist Level, he gives her a verbal look through his Day Timer and begins: "At 8:00 A.M. I had a meeting with . . ." The person who lives at this level finds it difficult to say things like, "Do you know what I was thinking today?" He also finds it difficult to express his feelings about things. Unfortunately his spouse usually wants to talk to him at the Feelings Level.

Level Three: The Feelings Level

"It hurt my feelings when you said that to me," a wife might say to her husband. He would then probably respond with, "Now, there you go again! How could that hurt your feelings?"

Both spouses are talking . . . but they are talking at different levels. Consequently they don't understand why they are having difficulty communicating.

The Feelings Level is where the deepest communication takes place. Generally speaking, it is much easier for a wife to talk at the Feelings Level than it is for her husband. There are some marriages, however, where the opposite is true. Spouses generally operate at different speeds. The spouse who finds it easiest to talk at the Feelings Level can usually get there the quickest. This can make the communication process very frustrating for both partners.

A couple may sit down to dinner and talk. First there will be the obligatory Grunt-Level banter with all its social amenities such as, "How was your day?" and "Fine." Some couples go no further. They eat their dinner, then pick up their newspapers and begin to read. End of communication process!

Other couples start out on the Grunt Level and move to the Journalist Level, where they begin reporting to each other such things as who they saw during the day, where they went, what they did, etc.

Then one spouse may lead the way into the Feelings Level. "When I was at lunch today, I saw Barry and his wife sitting over in a corner eating together. They must have scheduled a time to meet. It was kind of nice to see that," a wife may begin.

After hearing the facts but not knowing quite how to deal with the feelings expressed at the end of the "report," this wife's husband may agree that it was nice to see the couple together. But he may also pipe in with something like, "That probably wasn't Barry's wife you saw with him. Did you have your glasses on?"

Although the wife expressed her feelings with a light touch as she related seeing Barry and his wife meeting for lunch, there were deeper emotions at play. She decided to express them. "It hurts my feelings that you poke fun at the fact that Barry and Donna think their marriage is important enough for them to go out of their way to meet for lunch!" She even gets a little emotional as she expresses those feelings. Her husband, seated across from her, looks puzzled.

But He Doesn't Know the Baton Is Coming

"Where did that come from?" this husband might say, or at
least think. After all, he was just joking . . . wasn't he? His
wife reported seeing Barry and his wife having lunch and he
said something humorous about it . . . and now he had hurt
her feelings! This was just incredible!

The problem here is that this couple had been talking at
the Journalist Level. She was just reporting what she saw. He was
just reacting with humor. The problem is that, without warning, she had shifted to the Feelings Level. Now she was no
longer reporting. She was sharing how what she had observed
about Barry and Donna made her *feel*. He didn't jump up to the
more serious Feelings Level. Consequently the communication
between them was lost.

When this wife attempted to get her husband to understand her feelings with this very light statement, she should
have realized that he wasn't following her onto the Feelings
Level. He was still eating his food, joking around, and only half
listening to the conversation. He had not picked up on the fact
that she was really wistfully saying that she wished they could
do the same for lunch one day.

When I was a freshman in college I was on the track team.
The coaches kept trying to find an event I could excel at. Once
during the time trials in the mile relay, I was assigned to be the
second man to run the quarter-mile sprint. The first sprinter
came around the turn and into the area where he would pass
the baton to me. I was so excited that I just took off . . . for-
getting that I had to receive the baton from him! Without the
baton, all was lost.

The same is true when it comes to jumping from one level
to the next while communicating. If your partner doesn't receive
the "baton," don't try to go any further. It won't work unless you
stop and see to it that your partner understands that the baton
has been passed. See to it that your partner understands that the
conversation has progressed to the next communication level.

How Could She Have Done It Better?

Let's replay that scene. A husband and wife are sitting at the dinner table. They get past the Grunt Level and enter into the Journalist Level. At this time she mentions that she saw Barry and his wife at lunch. Then she ventures into the Feelings Zone. "It was kind of nice to see that," she says. Her husband misses the transition and makes a joke about the fact that it probably wasn't Barry's wife.

This is when the wife needs to drop back and reenter the Feelings Zone rather than attempting to go even deeper into it. This is no time to get emotional and say that her feelings are hurt. It's not her husband's fault that he didn't know the conversation was entering the third level. He was not able to get there as quickly as his wife.

"It would be fun for us to figure out a way to meet for lunch every now and then," she might begin again. "I would love to be able to see you in the middle of my day. In fact, it would *make* my day!"

"You know how hard it would be for us to do that," her husband may remark, staying in the reporting mode a little longer. "We don't work in the same part of town like Barry and his wife do."

Rather than giving up and dropping back to the Journalist Level, she stays with it on the Feelings Level. "I guess that's why it would mean even more to me, because I know how hard it would be for us to get together. This is going to sound silly to you, but it's not just the time together at a lunch that would make me feel special. It's more the fact that we went to the trouble to get together. That would make me feel like it was very important for you to be with me."

Then she thinks of a way to get him out of his logistical, Journalist Level and onto the Feelings Level. "Let me ask you a question. How would it make you feel if we didn't meet midway between our offices, but instead I came to your office? How would it make you feel if I went to all that trouble just to have lunch with you?" Now she was eliciting some feelings from her husband!

These Feelings-Level expressions come very easily for some people while they are much more difficult for others. This husband may still not be comfortable with the Feelings Level of communication, but his wife has made a start. Rather than letting herself get frustrated when her husband did not jump right into the Feelings Level, this wife took time to work on bridging the gap.

Watch Your Speed

When I saw Mrs. Smith, I asked, "How are you today?" "Horrible!" she responded. I was grunting and she was feeling! The jump was too difficult for me to make. I didn't know what to do!

Sometimes husbands and wives see each other for the first time during the day at dinner, when they are ready to travel at different speeds. He just wants to sit and relax and work slowly into the conversation. Eventually he will actually communicate . . . but not immediately. She, on the other hand, is ready to jump into the Feelings Level. He can't follow because he's not ready for that level quite yet. Communication breaks down if neither partner is willing to travel at the other person's speed. Communication won't work until the person who can reach the Feelings Level more easily is willing to slow down long enough for the other person to catch up.

Communication between couples is like running a relay race. Each runner must take into account the strengths and weaknesses of his or her partner because that person must receive the baton in order for the communication process to continue. Couples who ignore the way the other person runs will probably not win the race because winning requires teamwork.

Summary

1. There are three basic levels at which most people communicate.

2. The most basic level is the Grunt Level, where simple obligatory responses take place.

3. At the Journalist Level, people report facts and opinions.

4. The deepest level is the Feelings Level, where couples share how they feel about life and each other.

Communication Keys

1. As a couple, discuss the levels of communication that you most generally reach when talking together. Which one of you is able to get to the Feelings Level first?

2. Ask each other some Feelings Level questions such as:

   • "When do you feel the most loved by me?"

   • "When do you feel the best about our relationship?"

   • "When I am trying to talk about my feelings and you don't want to talk with me, I feel . . . "

12

The Genders Respond to Life Differently

We couldn't be more different!" Bart said, describing his marriage to the counselor. "Everything Leona and I look at, we see from different perspectives. Take last Friday night, for instance. Friday morning at breakfast we talked about taking a break that night, ordering a pizza, and picking up a movie from the video rental shop. But we failed to decide who was going to do what.

"On the way home from work we both stopped at the video store and each picked up a movie. Our choices showed how different we are. Leona picked out some incredibly long saga called *Anne of Green Gables*. If I had insomnia, I'd rent it! She's seen it at least ten times and the story never goes anywhere. The movie drags on and on about these people who can't seem to make up their minds about anything. It drives me crazy.

"I picked up the newest Clint Eastwood movie. It's full of action . . . "

"Yeah, and real deep too," Leona cut in sarcastically.

"At least they do something instead of sitting around, dreaming of doing something," Bart countered.

This couple thought this illustration was proof that they weren't very good for each other. In reality, all it verified was that they were very different in their perspectives about some things in life. Bart and Leona *are* different. He sees life through goals and pragmatic decisions. She sees life through relationships and feelings. They're different and yet each perspective is

118

very necessary to their relationship. What Bart and Leona are missing, however, is the understanding that these differences are good. Both partners need to reach the point that they accept those differences and try to "hear" them. Otherwise they are in for a lot of frustration.

The Swing Set

Several years ago a friend of mine managed the South Florida warehouse for Sears. My friend, Carol Manning, called one day to ask if I would like a gift of nine swing sets. I was ecstatic, since my daughter was three years old at the time. "Carol," I asked, "do you want me to come and get them?" "No," my friend responded. "We'll deliver!" There was something about the way he said it . . .

On Friday a truck arrived at Sheridan House Ministries to deliver nine swing sets. The sets were not assembled and were no longer in their boxes. The swing sets had been returned to various South Florida Sears stores, but Carol had assured me that the sets had been checked to see that all the parts were there.

The next day I met with eight other guys in the ministry at Sheridan House and we began to make nine separate piles of parts. Using the Owner's Manual we were given, we were able to identify everything and divide up the parts. Sure enough, all the parts were there.

As each man got ready to take his set home, one of them asked me if I planned to run off a copy of the Owner's Manual for each of them (we were only given one manual). Although we had already been through all the parts and had put them into piles, I figured that some of the men might still need the assistance of the manual. So I went to the office to make photocopies for each of us.

The next Saturday was the big day. I planned to have a swing set standing for my daughter, Torrey, by 9:00 A.M. The directions said to allow approximately four hours to put the set together. However, I figured that timetable was for average people. I reasoned that I should have this "baby" up in no more than two-and-a-half—max!

Why should I follow the directions? I was happy to make a copy of the manual for the other guys . . . but in my arrogance, I had left my copy inside the house on the kitchen table!

Three hours later, there was no swing set standing in our backyard. I had managed to assemble a couple of large structures resembling a pair of capital A's. But they were lying on the ground, slightly askew, alongside a pile of parts that I didn't believe were really a part of the set. Unfortunately, I still wasn't willing to read the directions. "I can do this!" I kept saying to myself.

Things got worse when some of my friends called to announce that their swing sets were completed. Of course, they wanted to know how my swing set was coming along. Rosemary told them I was still plugging away.

Finally I decided to listen to the one who knew the swing set best. I retrieved the Owner's Manual from the kitchen table, and by 3:00 P.M. I began to read the directions. By nightfall, one swing dangled from the frame. I would have been able to do more, but I had to spend the majority of my time undoing all those things I had done wrong.

Take Time to "Read" the Owner's Manual

My mistake with the swing set was to figure that I was familiar enough with the parts to be able to do the job properly without any directions. We often do that in marriage. The fact that we dated each other before we got married can cause problems. We may think we're so familiar with each other that there's nothing more to learn. Then we find out how different we are, and we dig in and refuse to take any advantage of directions. Who better to receive instructions from than our spouse? Our spouse is the only one who can explain his or her perspective. We must decide to listen to each other. The only way to understand another person's perspective is to hear it.

Understanding Requires Listening

A recent study has found that failing to understand the other spouse's perspective has caused many marriages to be rated as "unhappy" (E. C. Long, *American Journal of Family Therapy*, Fall 1993). One important key to the counseling process is to help spouses understand each other's perspectives. Again, listening is the key. The counselor spends much of his or her time restating what one spouse said so the other spouse can better understand what is going on. It's a matter of putting two people into a mode of listening so they can really hear what each is saying. When they finally hear each other, they can better understand their mate's perspective.

"Why is it so hard?" a man all but demanded to know. "Why is it so hard for me to listen to Colleen? I can listen to others but because we see things so differently, it's hard for me to listen to her. I end up talking before I think."

What a great statement! There are probably many reasons why listening to our spouse is more difficult than listening to a stranger or a friend. One reason may be due to a problem with the listening process in general.

Hearing the Noise But Not Really Listening

When are we ever taught to listen with our brains in gear? We are a generation that has been taught to listen while someone else does all our talking and thinking. We rarely get the opportunity for long periods of silence in our lives. Long periods of silence force us to learn to think. Instead, we are the generation of individuals who go walking with a radio/tape player plugged into our ears.

When I first came to Sheridan House, I arrived at the same time as another friend. Glenn Reese and I started at Sheridan House on the same day. Each evening after work, Glenn and I would meet to compare notes. Then we would just talk. I was older than Glenn, but I was amazed at how much more wisdom he had. He had an incredible ability to see things at a much deeper level than I did. He seemed to be able to see things from several perspectives.

One evening I asked him, "Glenn, where did you learn all these things? How is it that you are able to see the forest so easily, when I am constantly getting stuck in the trees?"

I'll never forget his answer. "It's because I have more 'think time' than you, Bob," Glenn explained. "You grew up in a suburb where you were always playing with friends, watching television, or listening to the radio. I grew up on a farm where I spent a lot of time on a tractor . . . thinking. There was nothing to do but think! When they started making tractors with radios, my dad refused to get one. I've learned how to listen and think. You've just been taught how to hear and react."

How true. Anytime I hear something that seems different from my comfortable view of what I think is the right way of doing or viewing something, I react. It's hard for me to just sit and listen.

Now, if a nonfamily member expresses a thought I might not agree with, I know how to just tune it out. I may sit there and appear to be listening, but I know it's not worth it to take that person on. I am not listening—I'm simply sitting there thinking, "Oh, you poor misguided soul!"

When it's my spouse or another family member, however, I immediately take that person on. Sometimes I don't even let the person finish his or her thought or sentence. I react simply because his or her opinion is a different perspective than mine.

That kind of reacting often leads to unhappy marriages because we don't allow ourselves the opportunity to understand the other person's point of view.

Spouses are different. In fact, it's *good* that we are different in our perspectives. What's *bad* is when we don't acknowledge those differences. What's *worse* is when we don't listen to each other's perspectives. What's *deadly* to the relationship is when we don't empathize or even sympathize with our spouse's different perspective.

Rosemary's Perspective on Christmas

"What would you really like for Christmas this year?" I asked Rosemary in September, thinking I would get a jump on all that holiday shopping. "Do you really want to know?" she asked in a way that was a little bit intimidating. It wasn't like her to ask for something outlandishly expensive, but . . .

"Sure! That's why I'm asking," I responded with false confidence.

"I'm going to tell you what would be the most romantic thing you could get for me this Christmas," she began. Actually, the mention of the word "romantic" caused me to become a little more interested in this project. After all, I did get her a little something from Victoria's Secret each year.

"The most romantic thing you could do for me this Christmas would be to take me out to dinner and then to the presentation of *The Messiah* at Coral Ridge Presbyterian Church." After she finished, she looked me right in the eye. The look on my face must have betrayed me. That's the last thing I wanted for Christmas! I know we are all supposed to love the presentation of Handel's *Messiah*. I know the *Messiah* presentation at Coral Ridge is second to none. I also know that when we went to see it once before, it put me to sleep! It was the longest four-hour performance (Rosemary keeps telling me it was only an hour-and-a-half long, but I don't believe it) I've ever sat through while trying to act righteously delighted!

"Surely" (one of the key words from a song in *The Messiah*) "there must be something else you'd like more than that!" I begged.

"You asked me," Rosemary pressed. "That's what I've dreamed of doing this Christmas—dinner out at a fancy restaurant and then . . . *The Messiah*."

Once again I asked her why she wanted to attend *The Messiah*. I was trying to discover what it was that I might have missed the last time. The biggest dilemma was her use of the word "romantic." How could anyone consider a night at *The Messiah* romantic?

Now Rosemary had progressed from the word "romantic" to the word "dreamed." That sure wasn't my dream of a romantic night out! There it was—our two very different perspectives. I know that we are different. I could ignore it. I could make fun of it. I could say it didn't make sense. But that wouldn't change Rosemary's perspective. Her perspective was *her* perspective. If I wanted to work on our marriage, the best thing for me to do was to listen to her point of view. I had asked. Now it was up to me to be mature enough to listen and sympathize with her perspective on this issue. Whether I felt the same way or understood was not as important as my acknowledging her perspective.

I really needed to listen to what wasn't being said by my wife. What she didn't say but rather implied was that this is what she wanted to do: Did I love her enough to hear it and do it with her? When it doesn't make sense, will I listen to what her heart is saying beneath her words? Will I take time to listen to how much this means to her? What her words didn't say to me was, "Would you do this for me even if you don't understand . . . ? Whether it is logical or not . . . ?"

You Can't Change the Differences, But You Can Change the Response

The fact that we are different is a reality. Nothing will change that. The only thing that might change is our response to those differences. Our spouse will be more willing to share his or her differences if we take time to acknowledge, listen, and sympathize. Sometimes we must even work at listening to the unspoken words beneath the words that are spoken. It gets old when your spouse ignores your perspective . . . or worse yet, after a while, a spouse decides that it's just not worth expressing.

I may not be able to change my spouse's perspective, but I can certainly change my response—that is, if I want to pursue a happy marriage relationship! I happily took my wife to dinner and *The Messiah*. Why was I so happy? Because it made Rosemary happy!

Summary

1. We marry people who have different perspectives than our own.

2. It's important to take time to listen to our spouse's perspectives instead of ignoring them or cutting them off.

3. Refusing to listen to our spouse's perspectives often leads to an unhappy marriage.

4. We can't change the differences . . . but we can change our response to those differences.

Communication Keys

1. List some areas where you and your spouse have different perspectives.

2. Discuss one of these issues by taking turns talking without interrupting each other.

3. Try to express your spouse's perspective.

13

Bring Notes

Every time Mike and I have our weekly staff meeting, something happens," Dorothy explained to her counselor. "I have so many things I want to talk about, but it seems that we never get to discuss them. Either he interrupts or I get upset. Sometimes I get nervous and forget what I wanted to say, or I forget what we really needed to discuss that week. Whatever the reason, I end up feeling very frustrated because we didn't get to talk about the things I had planned to discuss. Later on I remember what they were and get even more frustrated. I feel like we waste our staff meetings."

This problem is not unusual. Sometimes there is so much stress surrounding a marital staff meeting that the couple never manage to get to the important topics. At other times there is such a high level of expectation as to how wonderful this communication time should be that the couple misses the point of talking about priority issues. Often the staff meeting time is wasted due to a lack of forethought or proper preparation.

"Oh, I've been through those kinds of wasted meetings before," Mike interjected. "I've been through staff meetings at the office that were a total waste of time. We meet every Monday morning because we've always met on Monday mornings. Much of the time we all kind of wonder why we're there. It's just a habit and nothing productive is accomplished."

Distracted by Arguments

Why does this happen? There are a multitude of reasons why a marital staff meeting—or any kind of staff meeting—may get sidetracked. Emotions can play a key role in the breakdown of the communication process. Emotions can cause people to forget why they are spending time talking.

"I know beforehand that I shouldn't get emotional," Dorothy said. "But the minute Mike says something sarcastic, I lose it and shoot back at him. Before I know it, I have turned 180 degrees. I originally come to the communication table to work on the marriage . . . only to get into an argument and further erode it!"

Arguments shift the focus away from the topic at hand. It does take two to argue! One person must decide not to be drawn off onto the argument detour. Dorothy and Mike would routinely begin to talk about how they wanted to do things—how they planned to spend Thanksgiving weekend, for example. She might suggest visiting her parents. At the mention of her parents, Mike would make a sarcastic remark. At that point Dorothy would have to choose how to respond to his sarcasm.

Choice #1: She could become furious at Mike that he would insult her family and fire back with a comment about his parents. If she challenges him by making a derogatory statement about his family, the volley is on. Just as if she were slamming a tennis ball over the net at an opponent, he will invariably slam one back in her direction. The volley of insults will continue until she gets upset enough to storm out of the room. At that point Mike will slam the last ball home with a comment like, "See? It's just too hard to try to talk to you! You get upset over nothing!"

In the volley-type response, nothing is accomplished and the communication process is further eroded. This is the choice that Dorothy habitually made. She had to be shown that she has a choice about how she responds. She does not have to choose to respond to Mike's sarcastic comment with a "slam."

Choice #2: Dorothy's second choice could be to ignore Mike's sarcastic comment about her family. But this is easier said than done! To do that, it takes preparation. Before communication time, Dorothy must determine that she will not be drawn into a debate or argument.

When the counselor outlined these choices to her, Dorothy found that she could relate. Several months earlier, she had the horrible task of confronting a neighbor about something the neighbor's child had done while in Dorothy's backyard. This was a neighbor everyone avoided because she had a nasty temper. Before Dorothy went to talk to the neighbor, she stopped to pray and ask God to keep her calm.

Sure enough, the neighbor lost her temper the minute Dorothy started to talk about what the boy had done. Dorothy waited calmly and the neighbor finally realized that she could not draw Dorothy into an argument. The neighbor eventually calmed down and began to participate in the discussion. "Can you believe it? She actually invited me over for coffee later that week!" Dorothy concluded.

She knew how to defuse arguments with a neighbor, but Dorothy had not taken the time to prepare herself emotionally for the deeper times of communication with her husband. She needed to learn to choose not to become sidetracked during these times together by reacting emotionally and being drawn into an argument.

Distracted by Insecurity

"I get so nervous when we talk," another wife stated. "I'm not as good at discussing what I think about things as Ed is. Sometimes he makes me feel like an idiot for having the feelings or opinions I have."

Feelings of insecurity when it comes to self-expression is another way people get distracted. Some people spend so much time trying to express themselves that they forget some of the issues at hand. They are concentrating on the wrong things. That's easy to say . . . but much harder to overcome.

If adults have spent their childhoods—or marriages—feeling inadequate about the way they express themselves, they will expend a major portion of their think time trying to say it right instead of remembering what they want to say. Similarly, there are those who desperately want to avoid hurting another person's feelings. They work so hard at it that they, too, forget what they planned to say. These are two more deterrents to good communication during marital staff meetings.

Too Busy to Think

Marital staff meetings often occur amid a very heavy schedule of other important activities and events. It would be nice to imagine a marital staff meeting that is scheduled right after each spouse has spent a leisurely afternoon in the den, thinking through things to discuss. Too bad it doesn't happen that way! Generally a staff meeting takes place at night, after long hours have already been spent cooking, washing the dishes, conducting high-powered business meetings, helping the kids with their homework, dropping the kids off at some athletic or extracurricular event, and helping them with their baths and bedtimes. How exhausting!

If a couple waits to do their thinking when they are in the midst of their marital staff meeting, very little will be accomplished. Both must take time before the meeting to put their thoughts down on paper as they come to mind and think about the best way to approach the topics. It's too difficult to try to think of important issues while emerging from the state of exhaustion that normally occurs at the end of a busy day. By then it's too late.

This Is Important

Time spent in a marital staff meeting is important. It's too important to waste. That's why couples must plan to put the time to good use. Communication is vital to the marriage relationship. Each week many issues arise that couples need to talk about. One of the most damaging blows to a marriage is when these issues go unaddressed. And that is exactly what happens in many marriages.

When that happens, eventually one spouse will give up trying to talk at all. Usually it's the spouse who best understands the need to talk. This spouse quits trying to discuss the important issues because the discouragement over poor communication has become too much to bear. "I just got tired of getting my hopes up," one spouse said. "We'd go out to eat or away for a weekend together and I'd have these expectations that we were going to be alone and be able to talk. Either we wound up never spending time talking when we were together, or Jimmy would spend the whole weekend playing golf. Eventually, to avoid getting hurt and disappointed, I just shut down. I stopped trying altogether."

They Didn't Try to Make It Work

In the beginning of this chapter, Dorothy told her counselor that she became frustrated because she and Mike seemed to miss out on using their staff meetings to talk about the things that really needed discussion. Then her counselor asked, "Why is it that we seem to cover a lot of topics in our counseling sessions together? You seem to be able to come here for an hour and get a lot of work done. What do you do differently in your counseling session than in your marital staff meetings?"

"Oh, your office is very different," Dorothy began as her husband, Mike, listened. "We discuss this meeting on the way over. We both take this very seriously . . ." She stopped in midsentence. Dorothy had said it very well. She and her spouse took the visit with a marriage counselor very seriously. However, they took their weekly staff meetings for granted. They seemed to view the meetings as something they had to do but did not prepare for. Each week they sat down to talk with the attitude, "Well, here we are. What should we talk about?" That lack of preparation was killing the effectiveness of their meetings.

Have the Right Attitude

What were Dorothy and Mike doing differently when they were with a counselor than when they were alone? They weren't rude to each other when the counselor was present. They didn't say things that were degrading and belittling. They knew the counselor would catch them and call "foul!"

They also worked harder at listening during counseling sessions. They had learned early on in their counseling sessions that the counselor would ask them from time to time if they really heard what their spouse was saying. By now they were doing a much better job of listening to each other. That is, when they were in the counselor's office! Now it was up to Dorothy and Mike to take those improved listening skills home from the counselor's office and incorporate them into their relationship.

Have the Right Agenda

Dorothy's counselor asked her another question: "Why is it that we get through so many issues during our sessions together?"

"Well, I know we won't get to talk with you again for a week, so I bring notes," she replied.

Why not bring notes to the weekly marital staff meeting? When the counselor suggested it to Dorothy, she thought it sounded like a ridiculous idea . . . until she heard the counselor explain that his wife brought a small notebook filled with things to talk about to their weekly communication times together.

There are many things that pop up during a busy week that each spouse knows will need to be discussed. There are also feelings that are evoked during the week that occur at a time when it is inappropriate to examine them in detail. Putting all these things down in a notebook can greatly assist in discussing them later on.

People often become sidetracked, but notes keep a discussion on target. When notes are there to be referred to as necessary, it helps the discussion progress from topic to topic. Notes act as an anchor when the meeting begins to drift. The "anchor" of each spouse's notes will bring the focus back to where it needs to be.

With all that talking going on, there sometimes may be a tendency toward forgetfulness. Notes remind us of topics that may have been momentarily forgotten. When something comes to mind midweek, write it down. In fact, when something comes to mind midsentence, write it down! Those who don't write things down may spend much of their discussion time trying to remember what they want to talk about. If it's written down, one quick reference to the notes will quickly bring it into focus.

In the Right Order

Notes will help prioritize the issues. In the counselor's office, we always start our sessions with the less volatile issues to help everyone get comfortable with the whole communication process. The same is true for the marital staff meeting. Start with the least volatile area of discussion for best results.

Arrange your notes to help you create an orderly progression that will lead to deeper and deeper levels of discussion. A marital staff meeting may begin with a discussion of vacation or holiday plans. To some this may seem potentially volatile, but it should not be as difficult to talk about as, for instance, a couple's sexual relationship.

Use the opening minutes of the meeting to do a family calendar checkup. Next, talk about your children's concerns. Then move deeper into the discussion to include something that may pertain to the home or repairs or a proposed item to be purchased.

Finally it's time to talk about issues pertaining to your marriage. Progress slowly! Talking about whether or not to go to the movies is nowhere near as volatile as discussing the frequency with which you make love. Move slowly into these more sensitive issues. Put them on the bottom of your list. Just like it's done in business, use a written list to help you remember and prioritize what you and your spouse plan to discuss when you have your marital staff meetings.

Sounds So Sterile

"That sounds so unromantic," Dorothy complained. "I had pictured us going out to a candlelight dinner to talk, not sitting down and opening up our notebooks to give each other a report!"

That's a nice expectation, but it wasn't happening. Dorothy and Mike were not getting anything accomplished, and both felt like giving up. In their case, the use of notes was necessary.

Once again it's a matter of choice. Each spouse must choose to discuss rather than blame. Some people work at learning to talk about difficult topics. Others just create conflict as they battle over the same topics. Decide ahead of time—which will it be? How will you personally bring up the tough topics? How do you plan to handle it?

A Final Word about Agendas

It's important to note that the agenda must work for you rather than the other way around. Lawrence allowed his list to rule his weekly marital staff meeting. "We don't have enough time to spend on just this one thing," he told his wife. "We've only got thirty minutes left to talk about six more things!" The minute he finished saying it, they both looked at each other and burst out laughing. They realized how foolish it sounded to act as if the world would end if they kept talking longer than their allotted time, or if they didn't get to everything on the list. Use the list . . . don't be used by it!

Summary

1. Take the weekly marital staff meetings seriously.
2. Decide ahead of time to have the right attitude.
3. Develop a written agenda, starting with less volatile topics first.
4. Decide not to argue with your spouse, no matter what.

Communication Keys

1. Write down what you and your spouse would like to discuss at your next marital staff meeting.
2. Organize the topics.
3. Keep the notes near your calendar and bring them to your meetings.

Part 4

OVERCOMING
COMMUNICATION
OBSTACLES
BETWEEN SPOUSES

14

Opening Up a Shellfish

This sounds so good when we talk about it in your office or at one of your seminars, but when we are together it just doesn't work," a wife complained as she vented her frustration in the counselor's office.

"What happens?" the counselor asked both husband and wife.

After a long silence, the wife exclaimed, "This! *This* is what happens. Absolutely nothing! He never talks. We sit in the car or at a restaurant and I do all the talking. If I ask him a direct question, he gives a direct, one-word answer. Usually it amounts to 'I don't care—whatever you want.' It makes me crazy! I feel like I'm trying to carry on a conversation with a stone! No, better yet, a shellfish! I know there's someone in there, but I can't get him to come out."

In most marriages, each spouse falls into a "communication role." One spouse usually dominates while the other quite naturally assumes a more passive communication role. Some people fall into their roles out of comfort, some due to past history, and others out of a need to survive. There is certainly no need for both spouses to make sure that they talk for the same amount of time. On the other hand, when these dominant and passive roles are performed to the extreme, it usually means that one person is no longer talking.

Spouses Usually Go Where They Fit

When we bought our new house in South Florida, I was very excited about the fact that it had a two-car garage. Our previous house had a one-car garage, and that meant my car always stayed in the driveway, unprotected from the weather. That's no big deal, but I had always thought it would be nice to get my car out of the blazing sun and into a garage.

No sooner had we moved into the house than I began to have to deal with another problem. South Florida homes don't have basements like those in other parts of the country. That means the only place to store things such as bicycles, sports equipment, and lawn equipment is—you guessed it—in the garage. I gave the family lots of lectures about putting everything back into the garage, right up against the wall, so there would be room enough for two cars.

But it didn't take long for me to realize that two cars were a tight squeeze in our new two-car garage. Perhaps it could be done, but not without a lot of effort, agony, and countless lectures on my part. Even then, it seemed that the paint on my car was often getting chipped by bicycle handlebars and other objects. Getting my car under cover just wasn't worth it. It was so much easier to park it in the driveway.

The same is true for many couples' marital communication. Only one voice seems to fit. Though the silent partner has an option, he or she often finds it easier not to talk. It saves the agony of "nicking the paint" when the doors of communication are opened. Many couples reach an unspoken arrangement in which it seems easier for one partner to do all of the talking and most of the decision making.

But it's not really easier when one partner does all the talking—it's just momentarily more convenient. No arguments ensue. But it causes tremendous frustration on the part of each spouse and the relationship as a whole. The verbal spouse can be made to feel as if he or she is all alone in the marriage. "If he or she really cared about our marriage, he or she would talk to me!" The verbally passive spouse is left to find other ways of communicating his or her needs and opinions.

Even though a person chooses not to talk, there are ways to get across the opinions he or she feels are important. These ways are often unconstructive. They include complaining, one-line nagging, boycotting events such as family gatherings, or just escaping into television, sports, or hobbies. Everyone will find a way to communicate. Some just resort to nonverbal, often harmful means of getting their points across. The ultimate form of nonverbal, harmful communication can be manifested in various forms of abuse.

This marital communication arrangement or the roles some couples assume when communicating are sometimes only evidenced in marriage. A man who has become somewhat passive in the marital communication process may also be a captain of industry. There may be nothing passive about him when it comes to the way he communicates in the business world. He knows how to do his "business job." The "marriage job," however, is more difficult. If he hasn't had the necessary training, he may not be able to perform that job well. And if he can't perform well, why bother at all? The fact that a man or woman is a good communicator in the outside world often has little or nothing to do with how well he or she communicates at home.

Before looking at ways to open up a shellfish, it may be helpful to see what causes the shell to form around the hearts of shellfish spouses. Why is it that their heart doesn't seem to be connected to their mouth? Why are some people so closed to communication?

Past History

Some spouses come into the marriage with years of pearl-like sediment built around their hearts. That shell didn't just materialize. Past history has played a very key role in developing that shell.

As has been stated in previous chapters, there are many people who grow up never having seen the communication process taking place around them. They never saw their parents sit on the porch and talk. Not having observed the communication process makes them wonder why communicating with their spouse is so important. One husband stated, "What's all this stuff about talking?" He was as serious as he could be. He had never seen it done, so he had no way of understanding its necessity. Yet there he was, sitting in a counselor's office, trying to find out why he was so lonely, even though he'd been married for years.

Others have had childhoods in which their dreams and expectations were destroyed by parents who were too busy to parent. Many children developed shells around their hearts because they grew up trying to find love by pursuing a relationship with their parents, who seemed uninterested in reciprocating. When their parents bought them material things instead of spending time with them, the whole idea of continuing to pursue a relationship with their parents became too risky. "I tried my whole life to get my dad to notice me," one man said. "It just became safer to close the door and not let anyone in. I got tired of crying when Dad didn't have time to show up for my school activities. Now I've got someone [his wife] who wants to come into my life and listen to me, and I feel like I'm having to learn to open up for the first time. It feels very risky . . . very scary!"

Previous adult relationships can also close the doors of communication. Many people in second marriages find they have a hard time risking communication at deep levels. A previous failed marriage tore their hearts out. The fact that they risked sharing with another person and that relationship went sour caused tremendous pain. The pain was—and often still is—so great that they find it difficult to really open up and allow their new spouse the opportunity to inflict that kind of pain.

Without realizing it, some spouses in second marriages have made a subconscious decision. They have closed their shells and attempt to exist in the second marriage on only the most superficial levels. They want to have fun and relate to their new spouse, but they don't want deep communication—at least nothing deep when it comes to sharing their pain. *Perhaps a nice surface relationship in this second marriage would be more comfortable*, some of these individuals think. Once again it's a matter of deciding whether or not to risk. Opening up is always risky for a shellfish spouse. After all, there may be a "predator" looming out there!

Present Relationship

Elements in a current relationship can also cause a person to close up his or her communication shell. Perhaps circumstances or events have caused a spouse pain, or perhaps this spouse perceives that no one seems to be listening . . . so why bother talking?

"It doesn't do any good anyway," the shellfish husband told the counselor. "She wants me to say something or make a decision, and then she just goes on as if I haven't said a thing. What good is it for me to give an opinion that will only be ignored? My opinions are generally irrelevant to this family, so why bother?"

When talking and sharing opinions doesn't do any good, a spouse can become conditioned to closing up. When giving an opinion about something is perceived as a waste of time, a spouse can begin to wonder, "Why expend the energy?"

Worse yet is the spouse who won't tolerate a differing opinion. In that case, it may often seem easier to keep silent than to speak. It saves a lot of arguing.

"She asked what I wanted to do on Friday night," a husband explained. "When I told her I'd like to just stay home and take a break, she blew up! It's so much easier to respond to her question with, 'What would you like to do?' That's what she really wants anyway. She doesn't want to know what I want to do. I've learned that from experience. She wants to see if I can guess what she wants to do. When I answer with something that differs from her desires, I pay."

Painful events, such as marital infidelity (which will be dealt with in another chapter), can also cause one spouse to close up like a shellfish. The pain of the violation to the marriage can rape a relationship and cause the offended spouse to close up. Trust is a very important doorway to communication. If a person cannot trust his or her spouse with the marriage commitment, it's hard to risk trusting the inner thoughts of the heart. The violation of marital infidelity takes a long time to overcome. It takes a long period of trust building and forgiving to open the doors of communication once more.

For other spouses, the communication process only seems to validate their inabilities. As one spouse put it, "When we talk it makes me feel so inadequate as a husband. It's a constant reminder of how poor a job I am doing at understanding my wife and meeting her needs. Sometimes I feel as if it would be easier to just ignore the whole thing and go on with my life." In other words, this husband was saying that he thinks he might be more comfortable if he just didn't attempt to talk to his wife. If he didn't talk to her, he wouldn't have to be reminded of how clumsy he was at marriage. Of course, if he didn't talk to his wife he would never develop a better understanding of who she was and how to be happily married. Their marriage relationship would only get worse.

It never helps to ignore the weeds in a flower bed. That will only permit more weeds to grow. Some weeds are ugly, and some are quite lovely to look at. But the trouble with weeds is that they sap the life-giving qualities from the garden soil and choke out the beautiful flowers that really belong there.

These are just a few reasons why some spouses become shell-fish. There are certainly many more that could be elaborated upon. Suffice it to say that spouses do not become shellfish without a reason. It may be helpful to find the reason why your shellfish is having a difficult time opening up.

How to Open the Shell

For the spouse who is the predominant talker in the marriage—and the one who is attempting to open up the shellfish spouse—there are some steps that should be taken. The first step in the process is to decide not to take complete responsibility for every conversation. Decide that you will no longer do all the talking. Your spouse has learned to let you talk . . . so it's time for a change.

Many years ago I taught a small graduate course on a college campus. One of my classes had a great potential for interaction, but the eighteen students in their midtwenties and thirties would not open up. My plan was to begin class with thirty minutes of lecture followed by thirty minutes of discussion. However, during discussion time the students just sat there . . . mute. I asked a friend of mine who was one of the most popular professors on campus to sit in on the class and advise me how to motivate my students to talk. He sat at the back of the room and observed. Then he gave me an eye-opening evaluation.

"They don't need to talk," my friend, Jack, observed at dinner later that night. "You've taught them that if they don't take responsibility for their part in the class discussion, you will jump in and do all the work for them."

"Do you think I should start grading them according to their participation in the discussion?" I asked Jack.

"You could do that," he responded. "But there's a better way."

I was all ears. I was ready to hear my friend's innovative technique for motivating my students to interact in class. Jack stated it in just a few words, but they were startling. "State your discussion question," he said. "Then shut up!"

That was it. That was all he had to say. I'm glad I wasn't paying for his counsel! As I discussed it in more detail with him, however, I knew Jack was right. The class didn't have to buy into what we were doing as long as I was doing all the work for them.

The next class was a great test of who could stand the silence for the longest period of time. After stating the discussion question, I sat down for effect. Actually it was so I would appear more secure about this silence than I really felt inside. After a period of time, one student after another began to talk. Eventually they realized that I was not there to do all the talking.

The same principle can be applied in marriage. Although the silence may be difficult at first and may last through several marital staff meetings, stay with it. Decide that you will not allow yourself to keep the noise flowing throughout the entire communication session. State your thoughts or questions, then back off. The silence should eventually draw the other person out of his or her shell. Remember, your spouse is more used to being silent than you are. It may take a long time before "making noise" becomes a shared responsibility.

Don't Judge

Treat your time with your shellfish like fine china: Handle with care! Decide ahead of time not to judge. Sometimes a silent spouse will test the waters to see how sincere you are about wanting to hear what's on his or her mind. Handle your spouse's opinions, thoughts, and feelings with utmost care. Often the opinions stated initially as the shellfish opens up are not really his or hers at all. They are just shockers to see if you're sincere.

Before the next marital communication time, decide not to judge. Remember that the real goal of the staff meeting is not so much to solve problems as to develop the marriage. With that in mind, decide ahead of time to listen rather than judge your shellfish spouse.

Make It Pleasurable

For many passive communicators, the thought of spending an hour or two just talking sounds like a bad dream. Perhaps in the past such communication was a bad dream! There may have been times when even the hint of an opinion expressed by your shellfish launched the battleships.

How can your time of communication be made more pleasurable? One woman decided she would use her husband's greatest comfort zone. She asked if she could go fishing with him the next time he took out his bass boat. The thought scared him at first. He even asked, "You're not going to ruin fishing for me, are you?"

She refused to let him engage her in an argument. She went along with him on his next fishing trip and after over two hours together in the boat, all alone on the lake, both partners came away from the experience unscathed. He even *thanked* her for accompanying him! What happened to this couple who had been experiencing communication problems for many years? She made it possible for him to talk in a safe environment. During their time together out on the lake, it was possible for her to ask him to take her out to dinner so they could continue their conversation. All the while, however, she was aware of the fact that his availability to this whole staff-meeting concept was predicated on their previous communication experience. She had worked hard at making the communication process pleasurable for her shellfish spouse.

"I'm not doing that!" one wife objected. "That sounds so demeaning to have to jump into his world just to get his attention. Next you'll want me to join his softball team!" It's amazing what we will do for the babies we love. We'll change those nasty diapers and even stay up all night. We'll meet that baby at the point of his or her need because we absolutely love that baby! We must love our mates with the same vitality—perhaps even more. It should not be demeaning to make communicating pleasurable, but it certainly is demanding!

Marriage is not a fifty-fifty relationship—it's a commitment. And that means we must go to whatever length it takes to meet the other person. It means giving ourselves 100 percent without waiting for our spouses to meet us halfway. We must meet them where they are most comfortable and make it pleasurable.

It's important to be grateful for small steps. We often want to see huge strides of progress in the things we work the hardest at. Sometimes those expectations are very unrealistic. If it took five or fifty years to close those communication doors so tightly, it will obviously take more than a few months to crack them open. And there will most likely be some setbacks.

Don't let the setbacks destroy your efforts to open those doors. One great time of communicating without argument or sarcastic remarks may be followed by a month of very little additional communication. Focus on the positive times and don't let what seems like regression dim your vision for improved marital communication. Be grateful for any progress, however slowly it may come.

The dominant communicator in the marriage will probably be able to process all that is said much more quickly than the shellfish spouse. That is why it is important to allow time for silence. As Rosemary and I have repeatedly stated, time is a critical factor in the marital communication process. You must allow your spouse enough time to think things through and process all that is being discussed. Those who find it most difficult to communicate often get into the habit of blurting out sarcastic comments in order to end the conversation or avoid a perceived confrontation. Allow your spouse enough time to get past those comments and to think of what is really being said.

That's why the marital staff meeting held while fishing was so masterfully arranged. Both spouses could concentrate on fishing as they talked. The pressure was off during the quiet times because both had something else to fill the void of silence. After a moment of fishing, the husband could take time to think through what he wanted to say before speaking. Conversation came more easily because he wasn't being pressed to come up with a quick thought or response.

Guard Your Spouse's Heart

When a spouse risks coming out of his or her shell to express thoughts and ideas, it is very important that the other spouse protect that vulnerability. If one spouse shares the fact that he really doesn't know how to do this thing called "marriage," that he doesn't know how to sit and talk or even be romantic, it's very risky. The other spouse must guard that openness with his life. If that vulnerability is ever used against him, he will feel that it is unsafe to open up again.

"Ellie's husband is really romantic. Listen to what he did for her birthday," one wife said in response to her husband's comment that he would like to be more romantic for her. That in itself was quite a statement! But when she inferred that Ellie's husband was romantic, it was like driving a knife into her husband's heart. She meant well but unfortunately she took it even further. "Maybe you could have lunch with him and he could give you some ideas." End of nakedness!

Give tender care to the statements your shellfish spouse makes while coming out of his or her shell. Opening up is risky.

Guard what your spouse shares, lest he never share again. Don't offer advice unless you're asked for it. Just listen . . . and guard.

For the Less Verbal Person

For the reader who has taken on the role of the less verbal partner in the marriage, we would like to congratulate you for reading this book! Reading something like *We Need to Talk* that requires a responsive action is very difficult . . . and it's far from your comfort zone.

I know because I've been there. It's easy for me to talk to other people and speak at seminars for many people. It was a lot more difficult for me to learn to open up and share what is really going on inside me.

The first ingredient to opening up is a willingness to risk. We often grow up learning not to share our innermost thoughts. Opening up was once regarded as a weakness by some in our generation. But not opening up our inner selves can cause deep loneliness, even though we are surrounded by people everywhere we go. Decide to risk sharing how you feel about things, no matter how awkward it may seem.

It's not important that you understand why sharing is so vital to your marriage—you don't have to understand. You *do* have to trust! You must decide to trust that marriage offers an opportunity for a relationship that is second to none. Marriage is an opportunity to arrive at a "one-flesh relationship." Marriage is so much more than simply a sexual relationship, although sex is a very important aspect of marriage. It means knowing each other in a way that is more intimate than any other relationship. However, this cannot happen unless the doors of communication are open at a very intimate level.

"But I don't know how to talk like that," a husband lamented. I don't know how to talk about what's on my heart because I don't even know what's *in* my heart!" He was right. Too few of us take time to examine the contents of our heart. Special nonjudgmental times of communication that occur over and over again between a husband and a wife can start the process of thinking and sharing.

Find a front porch, a fireplace, or a diner where you and your spouse can sit and begin to think out loud. It will take time to get to know the contents of each other's heart, but it will also change your lives and your marriage. It will not only help you know your spouse in a new way, but it will also help you know yourself.

Risk sharing your thoughts. Trust that it is important for a husband and wife to really know each other and not to just live together. Marriage is much more than an arrangement between two people to share the bills, sleep together, have kids, and acquire material possessions. It's a lifetime of relationship, commitment, and companionship. Risk it!

Summary

1. Decide ahead of time to relinquish the responsibility of keeping the conversation going. Work at being silent.
2. Risk listening without judging.
3. Don't expect your shellfish spouse to communicate just like you do!
4. Don't give up when the process seems to be moving at a snail's pace.

Communication Keys

1. Do you do or say anything that causes your shellfish spouse to close up during the communication process?
2. If you are the less communicative spouse, what do you think caused you to close up?
3. What can you do to open up again?

15

Getting Close to
a Porcupine

Our daughter, Torrey, recently read *The Secret Garden* by Frances Hodgson Burnett. As she read, she would summarize a chapter for me each evening. I no longer need to read the book to know that one of its predominant images is a vine-covered wall. The young heroine discovers a mysterious key that unlocks a hidden door in the wall. As she opens it, she steps into a once-beautiful, now-unkept garden. The wall itself seemed insurmountable. But once the door and key were discovered, a whole new world was opened to the girl and her young companions.

Some people are like that walled-up garden. There is something beautiful inside them, but for some reason the beauty has been locked away . . . hidden behind a seemingly insurmountable wall. The door to the fragrant garden of hidden thoughts and feelings of some of these noncommunicators is easy to find. Others have learned to guard their gardens from intruders. They don't hide the doors to their gardens with decorative ivy that says very gently to trespassers, "Keep out, please." These individuals plant thorns around the perimeter to keep people from even trying to enter their inner world.

Rosemary and I call these noncommunicators "porcupines."

The Porcupine Factor

Porcupines are very intelligent creatures. They don't want to interact with other animals. They just want to be left alone. I once

watched as a curious young dog attempted to play with a porcupine. Everything seemed OK as long as the dog and porcupine
maintained a discreet distance. When the playful dog got too
close, he paid a high price. Without warning the porcupine em-
bedded sharp quills into the tender tissues of the dog's nose and
face. That young dog learned a lesson that it will undoubtedly
carry with it for life. The unexpected pain inflicted by those
prickly quills will probably deter that dog from ever again getting
too close to anything even remotely resembling a porcupine.

Many marriages are sabotaged by the porcupine factor. For
some reason, one spouse has learned to keep the other at a distance and away from deep personal conversation. If the more
communicative spouse enters the porcupine spouse's "personal
feelings space," the quills come out. After getting jabbed enough
times with these spear-like objects, the more communicative
spouse may decide that it's senseless to continue going through
all that rejection and pain. He or she may then give up trying to
communicate on a deeper level simply out of self-preservation.

"It's too painful," one wife described it. "Every time I think
we can talk and I mention anything even the slightest bit controversial, he explodes. It's gotten so he explodes more and more
often these days. The thought of even sitting down to discuss
things that I know we have to talk about makes me feel sick to
my stomach. I already know he's going to get mad."

Why?

Sometimes past patterns create porcupine people. Perhaps
these individuals grew up in homes where their father was the
absolute authority. Life in America was vastly different just a
generation or two ago. In the past when a father spoke, everyone
in the home was required to listen and obey without questioning.
Children were taught to respond rather than think for themselves. Many young men raised in homes like these grew up
believing that when it was their turn, they too would assume
the throne to rule and reign. Some children raised amid this

domineering system of authority said secretly in their hearts, "When I grow up, I will no longer put up with constantly being told when to breathe!"

Unfortunately, many who grew up in homes like these have gone on to operate their households with the same sort of dictatorship. Instead of responding to the problem by correcting it in the next generation, they carry it one step further. They rebel from an overbearing father by growing porcupine quills to protect themselves from their wives and children. Instead of learning from the experience of their childhoods, they establish their own kingdoms.

Too many times the patterns we detested in the homes where we grew up are the same ones we carry with us. Rather than sitting down to analyze what we are doing wrong, we adopt the patterns we saw in operation around us during our childhood years. In this way, the damage is perpetuated for yet another generation. The difference is that today's youth will not condone the dictatorship environment as calmly as the generations of yesterday. In the families of yesterday, the spouse and children of an unbending dictator just learned to live with things the way they were. They adjusted and worked around the dictatorship. Today's spouse finds it much easier to leave or to fall into an extramarital affair. Today's children find it easier to leave home, run away, join a gang, or turn rebelliously sullen. Fortunately, the world has changed into one where there are no second-class citizens in the family structure. Unfortunately, our contemporary society has made it much easier to leave these difficult home situations rather than to stay and try to open the doorway of communication protected behind all those "thorns."

This problem of planting thorny hedges around the walls of communication is not just relegated to husbands. Many wives become explosive or emotional at the mere mention of conflict. Though much of this chapter seems to indicate these porcupine communication problems belong primarily to the male populace, nothing could be further from the truth! Each of us has his or her own areas of communication in which we need to grow.

No one who is immature in the communication process can expect to get married and stop developing and maturing in the area of communication skills.

Walls of Avoidance

Most people in our society enter marriage without the slightest clue as to the levels of commitment required. Some people construct walls to avoid having to deal with inadequacy.

Several years ago Rosemary and I spoke at a marriage seminar for engaged couples. We noticed that some of the couples were diligently taking notes. The majority of those in the crowd, however, laughed at our jokes . . . and looked at us as if they knew *they* were never going to need this information! They seemed to be glad we were doing the seminar for those *other* couples, but they knew they were so in love that they would never need to worry about these potential marital problems we were talking about. Then they got married . . . and a few months later went into shock!

Marriage at its best is difficult. Those who seem to overcome the obstacles best are the ones who are able to admit they don't understand what's going on. If one spouse says or does something that causes conflict, there are just two ways to respond. One is to ask for information: "Obviously I've really done something that was out of line. What can I do to remedy this situation? Please help me understand!" It's the "teach me to be a better spouse" mentality. That approach says, "I'm very open and available." It's also incredibly mature. The other response is to build a wall. Rather than asking for more information or trying to communicate or work things through, some individuals determine that they would rather not admit they feel inadequate about anything.

Hiding from problems may not be a conscious act. The person doing it has probably found it easier to believe his or her spouse is the one with all the problems than to admit his or her own inadequacies. Learning something new can be intimidating. When one spouse suggests they go for marriage counseling, the porcupine spouse may say, "Why would I need to go for counseling? I don't have any problems. If you have problems, you go!"

If we don't talk about a problem, we need not admit there are things in our lives that need work. The best way to avoid talking about a problem is to make discussing it so unpleasant that no one would dare broach that subject again. One husband admitted, "I've learned that if I go ballistic, I won't have to hear what an inadequate husband I am."

"That's not what I'm saying," his wife cut in. "I'm not trying to sit there and point out your inadequacies. I just want to talk about the problems in a normal manner without yelling and finger pointing."

Even that statement made him feel inadequate. Her comments made him feel inadequate as a communicator, too immature to talk at a normal level. He felt more inadequate as a husband, and to some extent, his feelings were correct. Rather than inadequate, it could be better stated that he was unskilled or lacked knowledge in certain areas. Like many husbands today, he was seeking approval. Talking about issues like these certainly didn't make him feel he had his wife's approval. It was easier to avoid all discussion of what he viewed as his inadequacies by "going ballistic."

Resorting to counseling was the ultimate statement of inadequacy for this husband. Strained relationships from childhood created many unmet expectations that led to his building such a well-protected wall. Perhaps he had to deal with the pain of a divorced parent who promised to come for weekend visitations . . . but never fulfilled those promises. Or perhaps he had a parent who was too busy with his or her career to spend time with him. Maybe there was a previous marriage that ended in a crushing divorce. Experiences like these can lead a person to build walls fortified by thorns. A porcupine's response may be to attack when threatened by the next important relationship . . . namely marriage.

Porcupine people have learned to keep intruders away for many different reasons. It's not necessary that the principal communicator in a marriage knows all the reasons why the porcupine spouse has built his walls, hidden his door, and sur-rounded it with thorns.

Sometimes it helps to realize the partner doing all that ranting and raving is really not ranting and raving at you. Even though those porcupine quills may be pointed in your direction, you didn't cause them to form. It helps to understand that some past pain or habitual response shaped your spouse into a porcupine. As difficult as it may be, try not to take those sharp quills person-ally. Try not to defend yourself against the quill-like comments. Instead, try to work past your spouse's sharp quills to learn where he or she has hidden the door to his or her "garden." Watch out for the thorns!

Anger

When not dealt with properly, anger can become a raging bull that will gore the ones you love the most. If you become controlled by anger, you will find it will only escalate. Angry ex-plosions can become more and more volatile . . . until they begin to occur without much provocation. Anger allowed to progress to this point may require help from an outside profes-sional to deal with it most effectively.

It is not our intention to suggest that people who are involved in verbally abusive situations should remain there. Situations may arise when a spouse who is the continual target of angry outbursts should be advised to seek a solution that may include separation. The purpose of separation should be primarily to force the spouse who has become controlled by anger to seek counsel. Sometimes the spouse who has been hiding behind such a wall of anger will refuse to seek help unless the situation reaches such a critical stage that counseling is the only recourse.

The separation solution should not be undertaken without much prayer and counsel. On the other hand, a person should never permit his or her spouse to plummet to the point of con-tinual verbal abuse. It will usually just escalate. Separation may be the only catalyst to force a person in need of such help to seek the counseling so desperately needed. In the long run, separation may be what saves the marriage. That should be its purpose from the onset.

"How Do I Respond?"

"But it's making me crazy!" a wife told her counselor. "I want to reach in and find him, but each time I try to get him to talk to me, I always find myself getting blasted. How do I get near him?"

The spouse on the receiving end of a porcupine's quills should take a moment to analyze the kind of barbs being aimed in his or her direction. Some barbs are not as dangerous as others. If one can figure out what's coming, it's a little easier to handle. Barbs one can see coming aren't nearly as painful as those that seem to appear from nowhere.

Betty's wall was hidden behind thorns of sarcasm. When she and her husband, Steve, started to talk about their relationship, her porcupine nature would get in the way. As the conversation began to turn controversial, Betty would begin to take sarcastic shots at Steve. When Steve learned to anticipate them he found he was able to dodge Betty's quills.

"Six months ago, when Betty and I began to talk about anything that was the least bit disagreeable to her, the sarcastic comments would start flying my way. She'd say things like, 'Oh, and I suppose you're Mr. Perfect!' or other insulting things I don't even want to mention. Once she started, I would either fire back at her with more sarcasm or storm out of the room after saying something like, 'It just makes me sick that I can't even carry on a meaningful conversation with you!'"

"One night it all came to a head," Steve continued. "When those sarcastic volleys started flying back and forth, I told Betty it was easier for me to talk to the women in my office than to her. The minute I said that, something clicked inside each of us. We suddenly realized we were on dangerous ground. Betty burst into tears and I stopped dead in my tracks."

It was at this point that Steve and Betty came to a marriage counselor for help. They knew they had developed some dangerous communication patterns, and they wanted to work on them. When a counselor began to help them examine those patterns, they were better able to see what triggered them. That led Steve and Betty to the next important step toward better communication.

Don't Get Derailed!

When Steve reached the point where he knew when to expect Betty's sarcastic barbs, he could prepare. He realized that each time a conversation was perceived by Betty as the least bit threatening, she revealed her quills. Instead of responding in like manner or by storming out of the room, Steve began to do just the opposite. In the past, Betty had learned that she could terminate a threatening conversation by these sarcasms, but Steve decided that he would no longer allow that to happen.

He decided to let Betty get it all out of her system. He would not succumb to being mean to her in return, nor would he cave in. Instead, he *hung* in, and slowly over a period of months Betty began to calm down. She began to feel safer with him. Now she could risk talking about the conflicts as they arose without turning porcupine and striking out at Steve. Her quills no longer chased him away. She also learned that she either had to leave the room or stay and talk things through. She suddenly saw Steve as committed enough to communicate with her because he was no longer allowing the process to become derailed by her sarcastic comments.

After a while, Steve worked past the thorny hedge around Betty's "garden." He found the key to the hidden door in the wall she had built around her feelings. She no longer protected her feelings by sarcasm or shouting matches. In the past, when Steve had met her sarcasm for sarcasm, she had only felt less safe. Now she felt safe enough to allow him to enter her garden.

Stay on task when communicating with your spouse. Don't continue to take the same old bait when your porcupine tries to end the conversation by revealing his or her sharp quills. If those quills come out, don't be chased away by them. Eventually your spouse will either have to give up being a porcupine, get tougher, or walk away. Hang in there!

But Remember to Be Gentle

When entering your spouse's "secret garden," remember to be gentle. Many of the delicate things growing there have not been touched for years. The reason they were hidden away was your spouse's need for self-protection.

The next step toward getting close to your porcupine spouse is to decide that the issues you may currently be discussing are not as important as creating a safer atmosphere for future in-depth communication. Once a porcupine spouse sees his or her quills are no longer a deterrent to you, be careful to provide a safe environment. The end result of a single conversation is not as important as letting your porcupine know that it's safe to come out from behind that wall and talk.

It's Difficult to Stay in the Same Room with Some Porcupines!

When those quills are really sharp, it may be difficult to stay in the conversation. Sometimes it's actually better to wait and try again later. "I don't want to argue with you about this, but we do need to talk about it sometime. Maybe it would be better to sit down later tonight, but I really need your help with this," you might say to your porcupine spouse. Waiting a bit will give you both a chance to calm down and prepare yourselves for another try.

What happens if your porcupine refuses to come back into the conversation? When those argumentative responses are so ingrained that he or she won't talk about anything calmly, what then? Sometimes it is effective to express your feelings in a note so the argumentative one has no one to argue with. Notes have helped many couples with this problem begin to communicate properly.

Before continuing the discussion that ended on a stressful note, it may be helpful to write down the details of the difficulty that needs attention. Be careful to write down your thoughts and feelings without pointing an accusing finger at your porcupine spouse. Finger pointing will only cause further damage. Remember: be gentle. A great quote by Francis de Sales may help you: *Nothing is so strong as gentleness, nothing as gentle as true strength.*

Timing and Location

Again, timing and the right location are very important elements when communicating with your porcupine. Some people can have meaningful discussions the minute they get home from work and others cannot. Think about the best time to talk for you and your spouse.

Mary Beth made a very profound discovery about her non-communicating husband a few years ago. He tended to take out his employment frustrations on her each time they would start to talk on topics he didn't like. He would get angry over what seemed to her like nothing. She was searching for the best forum to communicate . . . and stumbled onto it by accident.

One night after the kids were in bed, Mary Beth and Allan decided to sit outside on the deck. She was wearing a very attractive nightgown and he was in his shorts. It was a very romantic setting and it became apparent to each of them that this night had the potential of being very special.

As they sat there, they began to talk about topics that could have easily become volatile in another setting. Mary Beth realized she had his full attention and that they were able to express themselves in conversation without becoming argumentative over every issue. From this experience, Mary Beth learned Allan was more receptive to deep communication when the discussion was wrapped in romantic expectation.

To some, this may seem manipulative . . . even demeaning. But it worked for Mary Beth. She and Allan started a valuable tradition of setting aside one great night a week that opened with several hours of in-depth communication and ended with lovemaking.

Sexual Frustration Can Play a Part

Mary Beth's illustration brings up another issue that can cause communication problems resulting in angry outbursts. Couples who no longer relate to each other sexually tend to be unable to communicate in other ways. It's all tied together. Sexual frustration can cause spouses to snap at each other.

Think of the stages in your marriage when your sex life shut down for an extended period. Those were probably times when you had your worst arguments as well. "Oh," she says, "but it's difficult for a woman to respond to a man sexually when he is not responding to her need for communication and relationship." Then he responds, "But it's difficult for a man to spend time relating to a woman conversationally when there is no relating sexually."

Shutting down in one area seems to play a role in shutting down the other area. Someone has to be the first one to give in, or the battle could continue to escalate. Each spouse could be waiting on the other to give in first. The man may decide to shut down verbal communication because his wife doesn't understand him sexually. She may decide she can't respond to him sexually because he won't talk to her without arguing. Then both become very argumentative. Now each has built walls and planted thorns to keep the other out. Someone has to decide to give in . . . for the sake of the marriage.

How Do I Change?

For the porcupine spouse who is reading this book, it's important that you know the door to communication can be opened safely. The very fact that you are reading *We Need to Talk* is an important first step.

The next step is to decide to risk change. Ask your spouse for help. "I know it's sometimes hard to sit down and talk with me," you may begin. "I don't want to be this way! I want you to be able to disagree with me so we can talk. The next time I start reacting to what you are saying by getting angry, we need to stop and pray." Your spouse may ask, "But what if you're so mad that you won't pray with me?" Those are times to ask for help. Risk setting up a way of signaling to your spouse that the conversation is beginning to get rough. Above all, the key is to risk! Risk listening! One couple said holding each other's hands across the table when they talked helped them through the tough times. They found it harder to argue when they held hands.

Whatever signal or technique you and your spouse choose to help cool things down, remember to have a willing heart. Be willing to risk admitting you may be wrong. Sometimes it's helpful to involve a third party in the process. A counselor can offer great insight into what is happening when a couple is too close to the problem to see a solution.

That hidden door in the wall surrounded by thorns can be more easily opened if opened from the inside out. If two people work together—one gently pulling while the other pushes—they can discover a communication process that is so much more rewarding than they ever dreamed possible. It's lonely behind those walls!

Summary

1. Learn to anticipate when a porcupine spouse is about to start aiming sarcastic barbs to derail a conversation. See them for what they are—not necessarily a shot at you, but a method of avoiding in-depth communication.

2. If you can anticipate those barbs, you can avoid falling into their trap. Don't let angry outbursts or sarcasms push you away from the communication process!

3. When the barbs stop flying, be very careful when that door of communication creaks open. Remember—there is delicate

territory behind that door. Your spouse may be fragile and easily bruised.

4. Each spouse must be willing to risk. What's at stake when working through communication problems with a porcupine spouse? The marriage!

Communication Keys

1. What are some of the more difficult topics of conversation for you and your spouse?

2. What do you do to escalate an argument when your porcupine spouse begins to reveal his or her quills?

3. Is there a good time or place to hold those discussions that would make your porcupine spouse feel less threatened?

4. Ask your spouse these questions.

16

Grabbing a Prairie Dog

Talking with Debbie is the last thing I want to do," her husband, Jack, confessed. "It's not a problem talking— it's just that whenever we talk, I end up feeling very frustrated. I don't know how it happens, but it happens every time. We start talking about something that we disagree about and the next thing I know, we're talking about something else that's totally unrelated. I walk away feeling like I've just wasted my time. It's just not worth it."

Jack wanted to be able to communicate with his wife. But when he tried, she would get nervous and change the subject. To dodge the real issues, she would bring up all sorts of things that he'd forgotten to do over the last six months. Jack might ask, "Honey, did you remember to go by the dry cleaners to pick up our clothes today?" If she had not, Debbie might counter with something like, "No, I didn't . . . just like last week when you forgot to put gas in my car and I almost ran out on the turnpike. I'm busy, too, you know! I have lots of other things on my mind!"

Jack had not raised the issue of the dry cleaners in a way that was offensive. He just needed to know whether or not she had gone to get their clothes. Debbie's response was usually an attempt to dodge the issues and turn everything around to prove Jack wrong. It was too hard for her to simply say, "Oh, I forgot. I'm sorry. I'll go tomorrow."

Other times Debbie would simply change the subject. Jack might want to know about an incident that hurt his feelings the night before. When he brings it up, Debbie may either get emotional and give an excuse or start talking about something else altogether. "I only said that because there is so much pressure on me right now. Do you realize how much I have to do between now and when your parents arrive?" In other words, the fact that she made objectionable comments is viewed by her as really his fault. She subtly turns the emphasis around to blame Jack for everything because his parents are coming for a visit. If not for his parents coming to visit, she would not be feeling such pressure and would not have said what she said.

It was all very frustrating to Jack. All he wanted to do was talk to his wife. But she continually sidestepped the real issues by pointing the conversation in another direction. Debbie could sit down and talk without any problem. The problem was, she refused to talk about the things that needed to be discussed. When a disagreeable topic arose, Debbie would disappear down a hole, like a prairie dog, and after a while emerge somewhere else, talking about an entirely new topic.

The Prairie Dog Factor

When I was a little boy we visited my grandparents' farm in Colorado. To a seven-year-old city boy like me, it seemed that my grandfather owned the whole world. He and I spent many hours riding horseback across his fields.

Along with horses and cattle, there was another kind of animal on my grandfather's farm that I found fascinating. This animal, however, didn't bring him anything but aggravation. All across his fields were little earthen mounds topped with small holes. As we rode across his fields, I loved to watch as little furry heads popped up out of those holes from time to time. My grandfather's fields were full of prairie dogs!

It became my sole desire to catch one of those prairie dogs and turn him into a pet. I remember planning various ways to trap one. But prairie dogs seemed impossible to catch. Each time I tried to put my hands on one, the curious little creature scampered over to one of those holes in the earth . . . and disappeared. I even tried putting a water hose down one of the holes, hoping I could flush a prairie dog out. I planned to capture one as he came sputtering up for air. Then I'd "rescue" him! But all the clever prairie dog did when I tried that stunt was to run underground to another hole, just out of reach. I could see his little furry head pop up from the next hole over from the one I was flushing full of water, much to my dismay! All summer I watched those prairie dogs scampering from hole to hole.

Some people have a very hard time talking about what they feel are the tough topics. Even the most insignificant ones, if perceived as dangerous, will cause prairie dog spouses to run for the nearest hole. They disappear down one hole only to pop up in another location. It can be confusing to their partner, who is really trying to talk. But the prairie dog is good at avoiding the topics he or she does not wish to discuss. These individuals give every indication they are able to talk and express their feelings, but in reality they only shift the focus of the conversation off into other directions.

Refocusers

Some prairie dog communicators are refocusers. They keep right on talking but work hard at changing the focus of the conversation. Rather than leaving the communication table, they just skillfully slide into another topic of discussion.

Dealing with a person who tries to continually refocus the conversation can be very annoying. A refocuser will work at doing whatever it takes to change the emphasis of conversation. Jerod was a young husband who faced that each time he tried to talk to his wife, Judy. If the focus of the discussion needed to be finances, Jerod would steel himself. He knew he and Judy needed to sit down and talk frankly about the family budget. Money had always been a difficult topic for them. Every time he brought it up, Judy would make a slight turn and refocus the conversation. This time Jerod was determined that it wasn't going to happen. He desperately needed Judy to understand their need to cut back spending.

Jerod brought this delicate topic up at dinner. "Honey," Jerod began affectionately, "I'm getting ready to pay the bills

tonight and we need to talk about some of the decisions that
have to be made. Right now I really can't pay all of this month's
bills."

What Jerod was getting ready to say was that Judy had
been doing a lot of charging on their credit cards lately. As a
result, they were in trouble financially. He didn't want to begin
by accusing her. He wanted to start off in a way that would not
cause her to back away from the discussion, so he began with
the topic of paying the bills. Judy saw what was coming and cut
in, "Speaking of money, did you know that Al bought Sherri a
new minivan? It's wonderful! They can pile everybody in for
carpool and comfortably drive the kids to school without all the
bickering I go through when I carpool in our old car."

In one second Judy had not only temporarily thrown Jerod
off course, but she had also taken a shot at him that made him
feel inadequate as a man. Her comment had subtly inferred that
he was not as good a provider as Sherri's husband, Al. After all,
look what Al had done for his wife! He was obviously a better
provider. He didn't need to have conversations like these with
Sherri about not being able to pay all the bills. He bought his
wife a brand new minivan! Judy, meantime, was driving around
town in an "old" car.

In the past, Judy's ploys to redirect the conversation had
always worked. In the past, this kind of refocusing would make
Jerod feel like a heel anytime he challenged his wife's spending
habits. After all, he reasoned, if he had been a better provider,
there would be no need to worry about the credit card spending.

This time, Jerod took Judy's prairie dog techniques on with a
new resolve. He had decided ahead of time that he wasn't going
to get derailed. One reason for this new resolve was that he really
knew he was doing the best he could to provide for his family.
He also knew that if they didn't come to some workable financial
decisions as far as the credit cards were concerned, it could do
great damage to their relationship.

Another reason why Jerod was so committed to keeping the
conversation on track was that he knew he needed to express his
frustration rather than continually allowing his wife to refocus

their communication sessions. It was the spending that was frustrating, not Judy herself. Judy would only be frustrating if he continued to allow her to refocus.

"It's great that Al is able to do that right now," Jerod responded calmly. "I wish I was in the position so we could buy one too. Maybe if we sat down and came up with a plan to pay off our credit cards and then started saving toward a minivan, we would be able to buy one like theirs."

The use of the word "we" helped take the pressure off for Judy. Jerod had shifted the emphasis of the conversation to make it appear that saving was something they both needed to do. He didn't point the finger at Judy by using the "you" word! "*You* have gotten *us* into credit card problems!" Whether that was true or not was by now irrelevant. "*They*" needed to work on the financial problems together.

Several elements made Jerod's approach successful. First, the introduction of a plan to save gave both partners hope. Second, Jerod sidestepped the "poor provider" comment, refusing to respond to it either emotionally or verbally. This left his wife with no further prairie dog holes to duck down. He refused to blame her for the financial problems so she did not become defensive and start to refocus. He, in turn, refused to accept blame for their financial difficulties. Instead, they would work out their financial difficulties together. Together they would find a solution. He let Judy know that coming up with a solution together would make it possible for them to replace their old car with a new minivan. The fact that all this was accomplished without argument encouraged both partners to stay at the communication table.

The Grim Weeper

There are many ways to sidestep the important issues. Some spouses don't change the subject. They get emotional. If he needs to talk about the family's financial state of affairs, she automatically gets weepy and expresses guilt over the fact that she just can't seem to carry her end of the budgeting. Some husbands feel bad that they have caused their wives to get emotional. They need to analyze a way to approach their wives when discussing these difficult topics. Failure to discuss them is not the answer. These difficult subjects still need to be addressed.

Whenever one spouse feels the subject is getting dangerously close to an uncomfortable topic, he or she responds in a way that says, "This is too painful for me to discuss!"

When talking to the spouse who avoids the issues by getting emotional, it is important to stay on task. Provide comfort to the one who is emotional, but don't let the tears be a deterrent to the communication process. Some spouses actually believe it's an asset to quickly get to an emotional level. That may sometimes be true, but not always. In fact, sometimes the opposite is true. These emotional responses could be prairie dog tactics developed to avoid talking about feelings or difficult topics.

In order to avoid talking about uncomfortable issues, some prairie dogs have gotten used to deflecting the discussion by appearing to show pain. The other partner must decide to stop reinforcing those prairie dog deflections. Once again, continue trying to talk about the real issues at hand until the person sees that it is necessary to the marriage.

"I'm sorry this discussion is making you emotional," you might begin, "but this is something we really need to talk about . . . "

"Yes, but . . . "

"Helen! You tell me you really want to work on this problem! Then you don't do anything about it," her husband, Phil, complained.

"Yes, but I don't know how to change the way I am," Helen responded.

"Last time we talked about this," Phil continued, "we decided that if you just grab a nap in the afternoon, it would help you stay awake so we could talk later on at night."

"Yes, but then the phone always rings while I'm napping and . . . " Helen returned.

"Then take it off the hook while you're napping!" Phil shot back.

'Yes, but then something else always happens and I can't . . ." Helen wasn't able to continue with her "Yes, but" excuses because Phil interrupted her. He immediately realized that he was enmeshed in one of her typical verbal volleys. He knew he was getting nowhere with this conversation. Actually, he *was* getting somewhere! He was getting so frustrated that he was being driven out the door.

As Phil and Helen continued to discuss the difficulty, Helen said she did want his help with the problem of staying awake after the kids went to bed. Phil let her know that she always seemed to have some reason why her problem was so severe that nothing would work. When he offered the help she said she wanted, she always found a reason why his suggested solutions wouldn't work. "Yes, but . . . " was her typical response to each of his suggestions.

There are many people who would rather talk about why their problems are so much more severe than the problems of other people. If they can keep their problems unsolvable, they can continue to feel justified in not working hard to resolve them. In other words, they don't have to do anything about their problems.

Phil had to talk to his wife! By now, it had nothing to do with whether or not she could stay up late at night. Now, it was because he was frustrated at the way she seemed to handle—or not handle—every disagreement. Phil had to learn how to get past Helen's "Yes, but" responses.

"What do you think would help you overcome this problem you are having?" was one approach he found some success with. When he asked Helen to advise herself, she often came up with an answer. Then it was his job to reinforce her response rather than attack her ideas.

Sometimes it also works to confront the actual avoidance response. "Honey, every time we discuss this you say, 'Yes, but . . . ,' and promptly tell me why each solution I suggest won't work." When her "Yes, but" habit was confronted by her husband, Helen realized she had reached the point where she was more adept at figuring out why solutions wouldn't work than finding a helpful plan.

Once the excuses are confronted, map out a plan of action. "Let's try this tomorrow. You take the phone off the hook, set the alarm for thirty minutes, and . . . " By mapping out a plan of action, you may help your prairie dog spouse past the obstacles so they can move into deeper levels of communication.

Sometimes one spouse just has to ignore those "Yes, but" responses and keep on going. Gently keep the discussion going as you help your spouse find an action plan that works. Keep the discussion going to pull your partner back on track. You may have to hear those "Yes, but" excuses for quite some time, but finally you will reach an action plan. When the plan is stated, it's good to continue the conversation a bit longer and talk about the plan. You must decide to act as if you never heard all those "Yes, but" excuses.

It's important to understand that a habit like this one is often formed by people who are afraid of getting hurt. Some spouses know they need to talk but are afraid to stay on a difficult topic for very long because they're afraid of getting hurt if they let their partner get too close.

Stay Focused

The prairie dog, or avoidance, habit can be broken if someone will choose to stay in the communication process to keep the discussion on task. The step-by-step process starts with staying focused and refusing to be drawn away from in-depth communication by the prairie dog spouse. Don't become discouraged and walk away or give up trying to help.

It's also important to be certain never to let the prairie dog's diversions evoke emotional responses. Emotional responses are often adolescent in nature. One husband said, "It's amazing! My wife is brilliant and successful in her career. She's mature in every way except when it comes to opening the lines of communication. Whenever we start talking about exciting areas of our marriage that still need work, she gets very emotional. I had to decide that I wasn't going to let her make me emotional too. She used to start to cry and I'd start to yell because I was getting frustrated at her tears. Not anymore! I had to treat this one area of her life as if she were still a teenager. I wasn't going to miss out on an even greater marriage with my wife just because of this one problem area. I decided to stay in the communication process and not feel guilty about drawing those tears."

Use a Hershey Bar

I couldn't grab a prairie dog as hard as I tried, but the clever little animals would come up to the farmhouse and eat right out of my grandfather's hand! Grandfather would sit out on the porch and I would watch with amazement as, inch by inch, those furry little prairie dogs would come right up to him. What was his secret? He kept little squares of Hershey's chocolate bars in his pocket. He never lunged for a prairie dog. He simply held out one of the little chocolate squares . . . and waited patiently. I never learned how many years it took for my grandfather to gain the confidence of the prairie dog population on his farm. Eventually, though, the prairie dogs learned to trust him so much that they took the chocolate from his hand.

It will take time and patience to get past all those prairie dog responses. It will also take persistence and determination. The spouse who decides to persist must refuse to be thrown off track or become frustrated. Be sure to reassure.

It's important to make certain that your prairie dog spouse knows he or she is loved and accepted regardless of how the day-to-day marital communication is going. If they feel safe, they may eventually be willing to come out of those prairie-dog holes and talk about the real issues.

Summary

1. When dealing with a prairie dog—someone who repeatedly dodges the issues—stand your ground! Stay focused.
2. Don't allow your spouse's responses to pull you off task.

3. Don't become so frustrated that you become emotional or combative.

4. Use a Hershey bar to draw your prairie dog out . . . and into discussions that address the issues at hand.

Communication Keys

1. Are there some topics or areas of discussion that you or your spouse tend to avoid?

2. What are some of the things you do to avoid these important topics of discussion? What can you do to stop this habit of avoidance? What can your spouse do to help?

3. What seems to be the most difficult area of communication for you and your spouse?

4. What are some ways that you and your spouse can warn each other that avoidance is taking place?

17

Communicating with a
Television Addict

All of this sounds great, but what about my husband? How can I get him to step away from all those weekend sports events on television? I'd love to implement some of these ideas in our marriage! But when do we have time for communication? He stays glued to the TV set!"

We refer to this couple as "Sam Sports Fan" and "Sally Sports Widow." Sam and Sally don't communicate very often. Sally would love it if she could get her husband to give up even one of his weekend games so they could spend the time talking.

But what about all the "Susie Sitcoms" out there, whose husbands take a backseat to the afternoon soap operas and evening situation comedies on TV? Susie wouldn't think of missing out on her favorite television programs because she'd miss seeing the latest developments within her favorite fictional families.

Both men and women can—and do—become television addicts. While men who watch sports events are usually the ones most often accused of being television addicts, in reality about an even number of television addicts hail from each gender. The reasons for television addiction are as diverse as the genders themselves.

Susie Sitcom finds her soap operas and sitcoms so appealing because they seem to fill a void in her life. While she yearns for a meaningful relationship with her husband, in reality her days are consumed with mundane tasks like doing dishes, keeping up with the laundry, and meeting the demands of a hectic work schedule. The soaps and sitcoms present attractive relationships in which exciting things happen. The intrigue intensifies and every dilemma is resolved . . . all within a sixty-minute segment. Unfortunately, these fictional "quickie" resolutions to life's problems give Susie a very unrealistic view of how real-world relationships should function.

Sam Sports Fan, on the other hand, lives in a world where he has few opportunities to win. His job is far more difficult and boring than he would ever admit. The issue of job security has also become more tenuous. It's nice to sit down for a couple of hours each week and root for a team that really stands a good chance of winning. In fact, the prospect of winning is so appealing to Sam that he finds he can do it all day! Even the sports commercials are alluring. In them, beautiful young women stand around, paying attention to overweight guys, feeding them their favorite foods and beverages! These attractive commercials draw him even further into the television sports world. Stepping over into it on weekends (and on Monday nights) offers Sam the pleasure of seeing for himself that sometimes people really do win. Besides, there's so little hassle involved in sitting in front of the TV set and cheering his favorite teams toward victory.

To the Sams and Susies of this world, television has become a great escape. It's a way we can watch people in very unrealistic yet exciting environments. We can see them win and succeed and prosper. On TV, all the police officers always get their man, someone always wins the game, and people always have passionate relationships. Television today allows people to dial a fantasy. Just choose the channel that promises to deliver what you want or think you need.

Most of us are probably not even aware of all the reasons for television's addictive appeal. Television is a hard habit to break, and it's difficult to draw a spouse away from the small screen. It's a challenge that will take time to overcome.

A Long Time in the Making

"So how do I draw my husband away from all those constant football games?" a young wife may be asking right this minute.

An important starting point is to realize that no one can draw a spouse *away* from something. You must draw your spouse *toward* something! It's better not to look at football games as something you need to engage in battle. Instead, you must determine to make your relationship more exciting and enticing, to draw your spouse away from the tube and back into seeking more balance in real life. Don't try to entice your spouse *away* from the small screen . . . work at drawing him *toward* the marriage relationship.

Many husbands have spent years—even decades—watching as their favorite teams play ball. "But with my husband, it's not necessarily his favorite team! It's any team or sports event! He watches anything with a ball, no matter who is playing." This wife must realize that those sports events have been her husband's steady companion for many years. He has even invested "big money" in keeping his "affair" with television going. When new sets with wider screens and stereo became available, this guy had to have one. He wanted to feel like he was sitting right on the field. Not only has he invested more on television sets than in his family's summer vacations, he's also studying to keep his information levels up. Each day, he devours the sports section of the newspaper. If he devoted the same amount of time and effort to the family's financial investments, the family would be way ahead. He's spent a long time and lots of money getting good at watching sports events on television. The habit will not be easily broken.

Going Head-to-Head

One wife's remedy for her husband's television addiction was to go head-to-head. She decided she was going to get her husband to turn off that TV and spend more time with the family—or else! Her approach was to compete with his television addiction. She decided she would no longer sit by idly watching her husband as he stayed glued to his games. After all, these were times when they could be talking and working on improving their marriage! She seemed to wait until it was time for a game to start to begin bidding for his time. Her attempts to draw him into conversation at these times were not accidental. She planned it that way.

She also planned family activities to coincide with his Sunday afternoon television sports schedule. As soon as she knew what time the weekend's games would be televised, she would announce that she had prepared something for the whole family to take part in. The activity would (coincidentally) start right in the middle of the game.

This wife continually put her husband in the position of having to choose. She wanted him to constantly prove that she and his family were more important to him than some old football game on TV. She forced him to "prove his love" by turning the game off to talk to her. And if he refused, she would gladly turn it off for him! When her plan backfired and he continued to watch his games on weekends and Monday nights, she "punished" him by sleeping in another room of the house. She was trying to compete . . . and losing the game.

This technique may work for some wives. In fact, that's why this wife chose such tactics. A friend of hers had told her that was the way to do it. "Get right in there and make demands!" the friend urged. "Tell your husband he'd better turn those games off, or there will be no sex for the rest of the week! That's what you have to do with men who act like boys!"

It may have worked for her friend, but this wife's husband would not give in as easily. The friend's husband was more like a son than a husband. Who wants to be married to a man who acts more like a son . . . one who must be punished and controlled?

This wife didn't want control—she wanted a relationship. She thought the way to have a relationship was to force her point. But she soon discovered that her way only forced a confrontation with her television addict. Her husband knew how to compete. He was far better at it than she was. One way or another, he would beat the system. He would either fight back and find another way to watch his game at home or go to a friend's house to watch it. He might even start going to the games.

Sam will fight back some way, whether passively or assertively. His passive plan may be to go to the family outing . . .

and take a small television with him. His assertive plan may be to tell his wife that at any cost, he will watch the game because it's one of the biggest games of the season. His assertiveness may even become ugly. Jumping into his arena and going head-to-head is not the best way to draw Sam Sports Fan away from the television set.

The Weapon of Guilt

Other wives use guilt to try to pull their husbands away from the tube. These wives work at making their husbands feel tremendously guilty for the amount of time they choose to spend watching what they term "the idiot box."

This wife may even go so far as to give the television the title of "Daddy's favorite child!" When the games are on, this wife works harder than ever around the house. She scrubs floors, washes clothes, and cooks like crazy. The best ploy of all is when she goes outdoors and makes a big point of playing ball with the kids—something she secretly hates to do. Each of these tasks is planned for its overall effect on her television-addict husband.

Perhaps she can make him feel so guilty that he will turn the television set off and get more involved with the family. "Why isn't Daddy going to the park with us?" one of the children may ask. "Why isn't Daddy going to the park? Because he's spending time with his favorite child," his wife will probably say in a voice tinged with sarcasm. What's she doing? She's trying to drive the knife of guilt further into his heart!

While all this was done in the hope that Sam Sports Fan would respond by reentering the family, his wife was furious that her complicated efforts had no impact. In fact, they seemed to drive him further away! To avoid all those "guilt arrows," Sam just went over to a friend's house to watch his favorite games. It had become apparent that it was no longer a question of whether he would watch his games . . . but where he would watch them. Would he watch them at home . . . at a friend's house . . . or at a lively sports bar across town?

Guilt didn't bring the desired results. Instead of causing Sam to change, it made him resent his wife for trying to manipulate him. Things became worse and worse in this relationship until the communication completely broke down.

Don't Run the Wrong Way

Spouses have undoubtedly tried many techniques to get their television-addict spouses away from the set. One thing is certain. The television is a very accepting, non-guilt-inducing partner. It's comfortable to be around and it never nags. Many spouses miss the joy of real relationship with their television addicts because they are using the wrong approach to try to get them to change. They're like athletes who mistakenly run in the wrong direction . . . away from the goal instead of toward it. Spouses who try to manipulate a response are really running in the wrong direction . . . away from, rather than toward their mates.

Jack and Fran live in our neighborhood. Both are big-time runners. It's one of the reasons why they love living in our community. There is a three-mile jogging path around it, and it's constantly being used.

Jack and Fran have worked out their own jogging routine. They jog at the same time each day, but rarely do they jog together. One day I asked Jack why he and his wife ran in opposite directions. "We both do the track twice and actually, we do it in about the same amount of time," he told me. "Most of the time we even leave the house at the same time."

Rosemary and I fitness walk the same track and enjoy some of our greatest talks while I gasp for breath alongside her! Knowing that, I asked Jack the next logical question. "Why don't you two start jogging together so you can talk?"

"That would be nice," Jack agreed. "Fran said she's seen you two talking while you walk around the loop. She even mentioned how nice it would be for us to do the same. But we don't run the path in the same direction. Fran goes into the sun."

As I pursued the conversation with Jack a bit further, I realized that he and Fran had tried to jog in the same direction and that each had reasons for wanting to go around the loop in the opposite direction. As ridiculous as it may seem to a listener, it was an obstacle that they did not overcome for almost a year. Fran didn't want to finish her jogging while heading into the wind and the sun. She wanted to get that out of the way first thing, while she was fresh. Jack felt that finishing the run facing the sun was the best way to build his endurance for the 10K races he liked to run competitively.

Jack and Fran saw each other as they passed at the halfway point. But they missed out on spending time together as they jogged because they insisted on running in opposite directions. Obviously one of them would have to give in if their jogging times were ever to become communication times. So far, neither had been willing to do it.

A Better Approach

The wife who had tried guilt to get her husband away from the television set made an interesting observation one Sunday afternoon. As her Sam set up a TV tray so he could have his snacks while watching his game, his seven-year-old daughter, Sissy, got a tray from the stack and set it up too. She brought some snacks, and instead of going outdoors to play ball with her mom, she sat down beside her daddy to watch the game with him.

Sam was delighted. He even went out to the kitchen to get a couple of Cokes for Sissy and himself. By the end of the game Sam and Sissy were curled up on the floor, sound asleep, Sissy's head on her daddy's arm. His wife took note. She saw that while Sam had refused to leave his world to join in the family activities she had planned, Sissy had successfully entered his world.

Some wives who read this will probably say, "I knew it! This is just a male plot to give my husband more time in front of the television! Now I'm supposed to join him as he watches his weekend games? Give me a break!"

Actually the spouse of a television addict will probably need to do a whole lot more than join his or her partner in front of the television set. He or she will probably have to serve him while he watches. Remember, we have already stated that the spouse who is addicted to television will find it very difficult to pull away from the habit. What the spouses of television addicts must do is to pull their spouses toward them. While manipulation rarely works, Sissy's approach does.

The ultimate goal is for the television addict to want more of a real relationship than the fantasy ones provided by sitcoms and sports events on television. The question to ask is, "Am I drawing my partner closer toward me and our family . . . or pushing him/her further away?"

The one who is more mature must take the first step. It's always the job of the one who sees the bigger picture to step across the line and serve the other spouse. No, this is not a sign of weakness! It's a sign of maturity. It's not a matter of winning through manipulation. It's a mission of developing communication so both partners can win. Someone, however, must be willing to start the process.

Jack and Fran are jogging together these days. One of them decided to give in and jog in the other direction. Now they're talking to each other as they jog for over an hour each workout. Eventually they negotiated a compromise in which they took turns running together in the direction each spouse likes best. But in order to reach that point of compromise, one of them had to be the first to step across the line.

Choose a Conciliatory Time

The wives of Sam Sports Fans husbands may have liked it better if their Sams had voluntarily left their games to talk. It may have made them feel more important. But they had waited a long time for that to happen . . . and it never did. Rather than continue to stand on one side of the line, waiting for their Sams to cross it, these wives decided to meet their spouses in the middle and choose a time for their weekly marital communication meetings that did not conflict with televised sports events.

If your spouse is a Sam Sports Fan, you too may try to establish a meeting time that does not conflict or compete with the games on television. Try to preschedule a time with him, taking his televised sports events into consideration when you plan. "Are there any games on Tuesday night?" you may ask. "If not, could we go out for a cup of coffee together? There are a few things we need to talk about."

Your mate may respond with, "Isn't your favorite show on Tuesday night?" or "Don't you have your women's meeting at the church?"

What a great opportunity to express to your partner how important his wife believes this communication time really is! Watch his reaction when you say, "Yes, but spending time with you is much more important than my women's meeting or watching a program on television. Can we get together Tuesday?"

It may mean that you'll be giving up something important for the sake of marital communication. But what is more important? Many spouses reach the point where they think they deserve to go to all those meetings or watch their favorite program on television. "After all, he gets to watch his games . . . what about my rights?" Remember, one spouse must step across that line. Choose a time that does not conflict with the games. Communication is the goal, not victory over football.

Look for Short Yardage, Not an Instant Touchdown

Be patient! When your Sam Sports Fan still refuses to schedule time to talk on Tuesday night, don't throw in the towel. Get into his world. Make some chips and dip and try to enjoy watching some of the game with him. Look for small triumphs, not full-scale touchdowns. If you wind up spending more time together in front of the television, count it progress. Remember, your mate has gotten comfortable over a period of many years, watching those games. Sitting and talking with his spouse is something he may not find nearly as comfortable as simply watching a game. Work toward short yardage gains.

To you, watching a game with your spouse may seem like you're giving in. But what it actually means is that you are showing your spouse you love him enough to spend time with him, no matter what he is doing. Step across the line and run in the same direction your spouse is running and see how your marital communication improves.

Learn to Appreciate

A few years ago Rosemary and I spoke at a church in Jacksonville, Florida. We talked about marital communication and the seminar included the topic of how to draw one's spouse away from the television set. One woman complained constantly that all her husband wanted to do on Sunday afternoons was watch a game on television. Another woman offered some advice. "Why don't you just sit down and watch the game with him?" This infuriated the woman who had complained so heartily. The woman who attempted to offer the advice continued, "You know, I used to feel like that when I was first married. That was before Billy went to flight school. Ever since he's been assigned to aircraft carriers and is gone for six months at a time, I realize how happy I am to be with him—no matter what. Sure, it would make me feel good if Billy would come home and just want to sit and talk with me. But I decided not to blow our time together, waiting for him to do that. When he wants to watch his games, I just sit down next to him and enjoy every moment I have with him. Lisa's husband's plane went down last year and now she can't even do that anymore . . . "

Every woman present that afternoon learned a lesson from the confidence she shared. Be grateful for what you have! Cross the line—don't wait for your spouse to come over to your side. Don't turn off the television, try to manipulate, or lose your temper. Be patient. Don't try to engage your spouse in battle or compete with the television. Try to coax your partner away from the television set by jumping into his world.

Summary

1. Don't try to compete with the games on TV if your husband is a Sam Sports Fan. Don't try to compete with Susie Sitcom's favorite program. It's a mistake to try to make your television addict choose between pleasing you and watching television.

2. Don't try making your spouse feel guilty. Manipulation rarely works.

3. Jump into his or her world and see what happens. Remember, the object is to draw your partner closer to you . . . not push him or her further away.

4. Be patient and count every small step as progress.

Communication Keys

1. What tactics are you currently using to entice your Sam Sports Fan or Susie Sitcom away from the tube? Are they working?

2. Are you doing anything to try to make your television addict feel guilty?

3. What is a more effective plan that may eventually draw him or her away from the television and closer to you?

18

Communicating about the Difficult Topic of Sex

It's Saturday night, the kids are in bed, and Joe is secretly hoping that soon he and his wife, Jane, will start heading up to bed to make love. He doesn't say anything about it to Jane, but he's hoping she'll recall that it's been several nights since they have been together sexually. In fact, tonight lovemaking is more than a hope for Joe. It's an expectation.

Jane, on the other hand, is absolutely exhausted. Although she enjoys their sexual relationship, tonight sex is the furthest thing from her mind. As they get out of their clothes to watch a little more television before bed, Jane provides Joe with the first clue as to her real mood. She puts on her worn-out flannel housecoat. She is trying to communicate that she is looking for comfort at this particular moment by putting on her most comfortable clothes.

Joe, on the other hand, was trying to communicate something entirely different. He went upstairs, and after a while, came back into the den, all cleaned up. He didn't just sit down anywhere—he sat down on the couch right next to his wife. He put his arm around her. Joe figured that she should certainly know by now that he wanted to make love tonight! After all, look at all the little signals he had given her. If she didn't know by the mere fact that it had been several nights since they had made love, he thought she certainly must know by the way he was behaving. He was acting very romantic, wasn't he? Wasn't he sitting close to her, with his arm around her, trying to comfort her as they watched television?

Jane noticed all the attention Joe was showering her with, but she thought it simply meant that he was very perceptive about her exhaustion. "He must realize how tired I am," she concluded by the way he was being so attentive. "It's nice to have a husband who is so interested in his wife's needs!"

Her clothes, her manner, and her lack of sexual response said everything . . . she thought. Making love that night was not on her agenda. All she wanted to do was take a break and possibly hug awhile before falling asleep beside Joe. Certainly he understood that!

Joe, on the other hand, mistook his wife's responses to his advances. He thought they were communicating on the same wavelength. That wasn't exactly the outfit he would have chosen for her to wear . . . but perhaps it was the quickest thing she could find. It sure would be easy for her to get out of in a hurry! All he needed to know, when he put his arm around her, was that she cuddled up softly next to him. Yes, they were communicating!

They had been sitting like that since about 9:30 P.M. Now it was approaching eleven o'clock. They turned off the television and headed for bed. Joe went to brush his teeth, came back into the bedroom, and got under the covers expectantly. In a few minutes, Jane came to bed . . . wearing her least provocative flannel pajamas. Joe knew that to be a pretty negative sign, but still he chose to ignore it. Finally he reached for his wife, and she turned toward him and gave him a quick kiss, then said, "Good night, Honey!" Preparing for sleep, she continued to cuddle under Joe's arm but things didn't work out like Jane had expected.

Things hadn't gone as Joe had expected either! He rolled away from her and faced the wall. He was furious! "How could she be so insensitive?" he fumed silently. His thoughts were so forceful he wondered if she could actually hear them.

Joe and Jane believed they had given each other all the right cues. But they made the mistake of using sign language. They relied on their behavior to communicate their intentions to each other for the evening. The problem was that neither one was "listening" to the behavior of the other. Each was too busy sending his or her own sign language. Reading the behavior of another takes a lot of concentration—something neither Joe nor Jane had been doing. They were so intent on getting what they wanted that they missed each other's messages.

Read My Mind!

Our purpose in writing this chapter was not to produce another instructional manual on sex in marriage. Other books have already been written on this very important topic. Our book, *Rock-Solid Marriage*, contains a section devoted to it. The purpose of this chapter is to relate to couples how important it is to openly communicate with each other about their sexual relationship.

Far too many couples play games when it comes to this all-important aspect of marriage. They use nonverbal signals and expect their spouse to pick up all the cues. They don't talk to each other often enough about sex, so consequently they are not relating well in sexual areas.

One of the games couples often play is called "Read My Mind." Without realizing it, Joe and Jane were playing it the night they got their signals crossed. Joe didn't come right out and tell Jane he wanted to make love because he thought as the night wore on that he had given her all the right signals. He wanted Jane to read his mind.

"Why didn't you just say something to me earlier in the evening about making love? You could have said something as we were getting ready for bed . . ." Jane commented. "Why do you always wait until we're in bed and then get furious if I don't respond to you? I'm not a mind reader, you know!"

Joe didn't like to say anything because he said it hurt his pride to have to, as he put it, "beg" for sex. He wanted her to be more perceptive about his needs. Jane responded by assuring him that he should never feel that he was begging when he talked to her about making love. She went on to say that because she wasn't a man, she couldn't understand his needs unless he told her about them. She explained how exhaustion shuts down her sexual desire. To Joe, being tired seemed to have no impact whatsoever on his sexual desire.

"You see, you have to talk to me about it," Jane added. "And it's best if you can find a way to talk to me about it before we get in bed. You say your pride is hurt when you have to talk about making love. I'm sure it's nowhere near as bad as when I fall asleep, never realizing that you wanted to make love that night!"

Verbal communication translates much better than obscure sign language. Joe had to learn to talk rather than assume that Jane had understood all his signals. But what should he say? Knowing how to talk about making love was difficult for him.

Risking Talk

"I guess one of the toughest things about talking to you about this," Joe said, making certain not to use that word, "sex," "is knowing just what to say. How do we have that kind of conversation?"

"Joe, it's not that hard for us to talk about making love," Jane responded. "We just need to be a little more casual about it."

"Oh, sure," Joe cut in. "At the dinner table tomorrow night I'll open up the conversation with, 'Please pass the salt . . . and by the way, let's have sex tonight!'"

They both laughed as they realized this was an area that needed work. Communication about the sexual relationship is one of the most difficult topics of marriage. To some couples, it may represent a great risk and they may even feel clumsy talking about it.

Couples are not usually sexually incompatible. They are sexually noncommunicative. They have not learned to help the other person understand them, nor do they understand the importance of listening to the other person's desires and needs. Verbal communication is the only way for spouses to help each other understand how they can do a better job of meeting each other's sexual needs. Communication is the only bridge there is between spouses' different approaches to their sexual needs. If the bridge won't connect, neither will the couple.

Sex Itself Is Communication

The sexual relationship communicates many things about the marital relationship as a whole. On a very basic level it communicates that a man and woman have a biological need as well as a relational need for each other. The man's basic needs can be easily communicated and fulfilled. The woman's needs, however, may be fulfilled biologically while her relational needs are yet unfulfilled. In that case, she many feel that her husband is communicating to her that he doesn't really care about her needs. Because her relational needs have not been met, she may feel by the way her husband handles their sexual relationship that he is only interested in having his needs met and doesn't really care about hers.

When a husband hears that, he usually says, "Wait a minute—that's not the way I feel about her needs! I want to meet her needs! I just don't understand them. In fact, they're ridiculous! She wants to go out to dinner on Saturday nights, come home, sit out on the patio and talk, then make love. Why do we have to do all those things first?"

Without good communication a couple may never fully understand each other sexually. Men and women are tremendously different. As this husband wondered, "How can I know unless you tell me?" His wife could have responded with, "How will you know unless you listen?"

Make Love Using Your Ears

The most important tool to increase communication within marriage may be a person's ears. Listening is desperately important so spouses can hear what their partner is saying about his or her sexual needs and desires. More than our mouths must be used to express our innermost needs and wishes; we must use our ears to hear what our partner is saying about these vital marital issues.

It's different for unmarried couples. They seem to be able to talk very freely about sexual issues. In fact, sex is a tremendously overworked topic. Why? Today's culture loves to talk about sex. Whether it's in the office, the locker room, or laced throughout an advertising campaign, sex is often—and openly—discussed. Unfortunately the sexual relationship is rarely mentioned between married individuals. Spouses find it more difficult than unmarried persons to talk openly about this very intimate relationship that was specifically created and established just for marriage.

When God referred to marriage as a husband and wife "knowing" each other, He meant more by that word than simply meeting each other's biological needs. For a husband and wife to know each other in terms of sexual intimacy involves more than just having sex. That's what animals do. That's why the Bible differentiates man from the other animals by stating that he and his wife are to know each other. To respond to one's spouse in a way that is more than just biological, he or she must learn to understand the other in a completely intimate way. The only way to learn is to be taught, and the only way one can be taught about another person sexually is to communicate about the sexual relationship. Only through communication can a husband and wife truly reach the point of knowing each other on such a deep, intimate basis.

Set a specific time to talk about sexual issues. "Setting the appointment to discuss our sexual relationship isn't the hard part," Joe said sheepishly. "It's getting into actually discussing the topic that's hard to do. How do we begin?"

There are several good books (see the list Rosemary and I have prepared at the end of this chapter) on the subject of marital sex that couples can read together to help them communicate more openly. We recommend that every couple work at continuing to improve communication in this very important area. Communicating about sexual issues should not be relegated to marriages that are already in trouble. Spouses should read these helpful books together out loud. Then the topics and questions should be discussed and applied to the marriage on a personal application level.

Joe and Jane may then ask each other questions like, "Does that pertain to our marriage? Is what the author suggested also true of our marriage? Would you like it if I were more responsive in the way the author indicated? Do you think you would like it if I did that?"

Use these books as learning tools rather than a means to indict your spouse or fault find. In other words, a properly written book can be used as a valuable facilitator to help a couple discuss the important questions that may be difficult to ask. Be sure to choose a book written from the perspective of your own philosophy of life. Rosemary and I, for example, would want to be certain that the authors were Christians so we would know they were addressing marriage from the same level of commitment and perspectives that we share.

As you read, let the topics evolve naturally . . . then discuss each one. Make sure you set aside enough time to read a section, then talk.

Sometimes couples cannot agree on studying a book together. In that case, one spouse may choose to read the book privately in order to become the best educated and most responsive partner possible.

While a book about sex in marriage can prove helpful in outlining various aspects of the sexual relationship, only those spouses who choose to listen will benefit. This is not a time for one spouse to explain his or her side of an issue. It's a time to listen to the views stated by the author, then listen to each other as each spouse discusses the feelings aroused by the material they have just read.

Try to hear your spouse's needs where lovemaking is concerned. Each person's needs vary dramatically. One of the greatest mistakes couples can make is for one spouse to assume that his or her needs are identical to the other spouse's.

Joe had strong biological needs. He was trying to communicate to Jane that he really looked forward to their lovemaking. His desire to make love as frequently as every other night had nothing to do with whether he and Jane were getting along well. Whether or not they were getting along was not a factor when it came to his sexual desire for his wife. To Jane, however, it was a factor. Joe's desire for lovemaking on an evening when

there had been an argument between them seemed insulting to
her . . . even animalistic on his part.

"I can't believe that we can be arguing all night," Jane
stated as if in unbelief, "then you still want to make love when
we go to bed! That's unbelievable to me."

Joe, however, had never connected their lovemaking to
the state of their relationship. To Jane, a good, warm relationship was part of sexual foreplay. Because they had not been
talking about their different perspectives, they had constantly
been missing each other's needs. Joe needed to communicate
with Jane so he could better understand her desire for relationship. Jane needed to communicate with Joe so she could better
understand that he was not some insensitive brute who simply
used her to meet his animalistic, biological desires. Reading a
book that pointed up their different needs proved to be tremendously helpful to Joe and Jane. It had helped them to realize
they weren't married to weirdos, but to spouses who were very
typical of their gender.

Jane painted Joe a word picture that helped him understand her need for relationship as foreplay to their lovemaking.
"You get mad at me when I take that rechargeable flashlight out
of the electrical socket to plug the iron into the wall outlet,"
Jane began. "Sometimes I forget to put the flashlight back in
the socket."

"That's right," Joe said, following her illustration perfectly.
"But it's because the flashlight won't turn on if it's not plugged
in beforehand."

"Exactly!" Jane continued, right on cue. "Just like the flashlight, I need to be 'plugged in' beforehand or I won't 'turn on.'
I need to have a relationship with you during the evening or it's
difficult for me to get excited about making love. You, on the
other hand, must have some reserve battery somewhere! You
don't understand me because you don't need to be plugged in to
the 'relationship' socket before we make love. You can turn on
instantly . . . anytime . . . anywhere! I'm not like you. You
can't leave my 'flashlight' sitting unplugged in the middle of the
floor and expect it to work later."

Communication of Desires

When discussing each other's desires within the sexual relationship, couples should make a great effort to find a balance. The term *desires* refers to a person's wants beyond basic sexual intercourse. This includes topics that often need to be addressed such as physical positions for sexual intercourse, kinds of foreplay, oral sex, and other issues in which spouses are bound to have different opinions. These topics cannot be ignored. For many of these topics, there are no right and wrong opinions. It is simply a matter of one spouse's desire versus his or her partner's opinion or feelings about it. Again, we will not go into depth or discussion on the issue of desires. It is significant to note, however, that couples must decide to communicate about these areas of sexual conflict. The desires of each spouse should be open for discussion and then dealt with.

The sexual relationship and the area of personal desires have become greatly polluted by our media and today's entertainment industry. Not only does the movie industry portray sexuality as one big, instantaneous time of passion, but it has also been responsible for many individuals having unrealistic expectations. Furthermore, today's hedonistic environment has caused the desires of many spouses to cross the boundary of proper sexual expression.

The sexual relationship should certainly be a wonderful time of intimacy between a husband and wife. It should also be a time when one spouse strives to meet the desires of the other spouse. It should not be an experience in which one spouse is asked to go beyond his or her own personal boundaries of propriety. One spouse should not come away from a sexual encounter feeling used or demeaned.

The sexual relationship is a time of giving oneself to the other spouse—not a time of taking from another. If both spouses desire to give themselves to the other—even occasionally beyond a personal comfort zone—the relationship may stay exciting. Giving also means *giving up* desires that the other spouse may feel he or she cannot fulfill. Again, there must be a balance.

Neither Rosemary nor I intend for this section about sexual communication in marriage to be used as a weapon to coerce a spouse into doing things he or she is not comfortable with. One spouse should not read this chapter and say to the other, "See, you're supposed to go past your comfort zone to meet my desires!" That would be missing the whole point! Our objective is to point out the importance of the giving of self rather than the forcing of another to give in. Talk should center around the thought, "What can *I* give?" For Joe, giving could mean something as simple as being willing to put on a tie before taking Jane out for dinner at a nice restaurant. He was even surprised at how easy it was, once he decided to give.

The only way to reach a balance on the issue of desires is through verbal communication. Without it, every lovemaking experience will begin with one spouse wondering if he or she will be asked to do something out of the comfort zone. "Will I be forced to do something I don't wish to do? How can I avoid it?" With pressure like that, who can look forward to lovemaking? The whole sexual relationship may be in danger of becoming something that one spouse would like to avoid altogether.

Communication During Sex

Song of Solomon 2:6 (NIV) states, "His left arm is under my head,/and his right arm embraces me." The word "embrace" in this passage from the Bible can be translated as *fondle*. Here is a picture of a woman communicating to her husband, even in the midst of sexual intercourse. What better time to risk communication about the sexual relationship than in the midst of it? It is important to talk to each other to determine the exact nature of the needs of each spouse. The very wise wife depicted in this Bible verse was telling her husband how to love her. Then she expressed to him how skilled he was at pleasing her. Don't reserve communication on sexual issues for simply a prearranged discussion. Communication about sex can be very helpful in the form of short, reassuring phrases during lovemaking.

Sex in Marriage Is a Gift

The sexual relationship is one of the greatest forms of communication a couple will ever know or experience. It's a time when you exchange thoughts and feelings with your spouse. It's a time when you can pay full attention to your spouse's needs. It's an opportunity to give yourself fully to your spouse. This cannot be done without including communication as part of the foreplay process. Without communication and a desire to listen to each other, your sexual relationship may seem awkward—a time of guessing each other's needs, and perhaps even fraught with feelings of failure and inadequacy.

Communication about the sexual relationship can remedy many of these common misunderstandings. Listen to your spouse. Then ask, "What is my spouse saying to me? What does he or she really want from me? How can I explain my needs and desires so they will be more clearly understood?" Communication on these intimate topics cannot be reached without a certain amount of risk.

Summary

1. One of the most difficult discussion topics in marriage is the sexual relationship. Too many couples rely on sign language rather than clearly stating the issues.

2. When God used the term "know" in reference to sex in marriage, He meant more than the need for a husband and wife to understand each other's biological and anatomical differences. It takes a lifetime of understanding and intimacy to build the marriage relationship, which is like no other relationship on earth.

3. Husbands and wives should clearly communicate their sexual needs as well as their desires to each other.

4. Sex in marriage should be viewed in terms of each partner giving to the other, rather than taking something away. It's

difficult to know how to give to each other . . . unless couples talk about these issues.

5. Sometimes a book about marriage and sexuality by a reputable author can help stimulate discussion.

Communication Keys

1. How do you communicate your sexual needs to your spouse?
2. How does your spouse communicate his or her needs to you? Do you always understand your partner's signals?
3. What are some areas of your sexual relationship that you and your partner disagree on? How can you best talk about these sensitive issues?
4. Discuss with your spouse your sexual desires. Then listen as he or she discusses their desires with you.

Further Reading on This Topic

Rock-Solid Marriage, Robert and Rosemary Barnes, Word.

The Act of Marriage, Tim LaHaye, Bantam.

Sex Facts For The Family, Clifford and Joyce Penner, Word.

The Gift of Sex, Clifford and Joyce Penner, Word.

19

Compromise Complements Communication

I remember how astonished I was at the many problems surrounding the Vietnam peace talks. I recall that it wasn't the process itself that I found so amazing, but the fact that the two sides seemed to have such a hard time actually getting to the table to talk! Both sides indicated they really wanted to talk peace, but from the very beginning problems arose that determined how the talks would be conducted. The delegates spent an incredible amount of time arguing about how the process was to take place—not the process itself, but its format. They couldn't even decide who would sit where! Even small details like the room where the talks would take place and how the table should be designed were discussed over and over again without much progress. Neither side was willing to give an inch on these preliminary issues. They refused to compromise on the smallest issues, let alone the major points. The lack of willingness to compromise exhibited by both sides proved to be a major deterrent to the peace efforts.

A willingness to compromise is a great ingredient to the whole communication process in the marriage. Too many times the issues of marriage and family are blown way out of proportion simply because both spouses have dug a great hole. Because of their unwillingness to compromise on even the most insignificant issues, they never make progress in the really important areas of discussion. Many marriages can't get to the "peace talks" because neither party will compromise.

Parenting Issues Call for Compromise

One of the most volatile issues between spouses is parental discipline. The parenting process is a great example of an area where compromise in communication is often necessary. When there is no compromise among parents, positive parenting does not take place.

Each spouse comes to the parental arena with a totally different background than his or her partner. Both were probably raised by completely different parenting techniques. One may believe that training a child to keep a clean room is absolutely mandatory for character development. After all, isn't it important to teach a child organizational skills? Doesn't it start with learning how to properly organize one's room? That makes good, logical sense!

The other parent may feel there are so many other important values and character qualities to build into a child that parents shouldn't go to battle over a messy room. If a child is continually sent to bed early as a consequence for keeping a messy room, how will he or she ever spend quality time with the family? Aren't there other, more significant areas of character building to stress in child rearing? Now, that makes good sense!

The problem is, both of these techniques make good sense. Both spouses have the right idea. They must either blend their ideas through good parental communication for a great plan that will really benefit their child or go to war with each other. If the parents do not choose to blend, they will try to *bend* each other. The couple who is unwilling to communicate and compromise will cause every member of the family to suffer.

Sally and Frank had this very problem. They had been raised in different kinds of homes, and each brought his or her parents' style of child rearing into their new family.

An Uncompromising Issue

Sally was very concerned about maintaining a rigid, structured environment for her four-year-old daughter, Ellen. To Sally, it was important that Ellen—among other things—be in bed each night by eight o'clock sharp. There was a routine that took place in their home each night after dinner that put Ellen in bed before 8:00 P.M., and Ellen worked hard to maintain the schedule.

Frank was not as structured in his approach to little Ellen's daily routine. In fact, he actually prided himself in balancing his wife's "lack of fun attitude," as he called it, with his fun-loving nature. Though unintentionally, he frequently interrupted his wife's carefully planned routine. He simply felt it was important for Ellen to have fun now and then. Four-year-old Ellen had already learned how to work her parents against each other. She knew how to please her mom, and she also knew how to have fun with her dad.

After Ellen had her bath and brushed her teeth, Sally would put her to bed at five minutes to eight. Once in bed and calmed down, mother and daughter would read a Bible story and say their prayers. As Sally left her daughter's room, it was Dad's turn to come in to say good night. The problem was that he stayed for twenty-five minutes—long enough to get his daughter excited all over again. Eventually Mom would have to come into the room and interrupt the two in the midst of their playful antics. After all, Ellen must go to sleep! Sally became the parent who always interrupted the fun. To aggravate matters, Ellen would say to her mother, "Oh, please let Daddy stay with me a little longer!"

This sort of inconsistency in handling Ellen was a constant source of disagreement for Sally and Frank. It had reached the point where they couldn't agree on anything when discussing Ellen's behavior. In fact, it even went a step further. When they couldn't communicate about parenting issues without disagreement, each parent took steps to counterbalance the other's behavioral plan. Rather than talk to each other, they took action to negate what the other had been doing in Ellen's young life. Each was adamant that his or her method of raising Ellen was the right one. Both were wrong because they were unwilling to take steps toward compromise or change.

When a couple refuse to compromise, communication is not possible. Instead of communicating with each other, they take action against each other. The action they take is usually destructive to the whole marriage relationship. Notice that Frank and Sally were not having problems with their marital relationship. Their problems were in the area of parenting. But because their disagreements over parenting had become so severe, the parenting problems began to spill over into the other areas of their lives. Now their marriage was in trouble because of their unwillingness to compromise on the parenting issue.

Lack of Compromise, Lack of Progress

Because Frank and Sally would not compromise, they were not communicating verbally. It's hard to talk when neither spouse is willing to give ground. Couples do find other ways, however, to send signals. Communication can become nonverbal.

One night Sally went to a Sunday school class meeting. The last thing she did, as she walked out the door, was to remind her husband that Ellen didn't need any more junk food or television because she was battling a cold. "Please have her in bed before eight," she said. To make her point, she exaggerated the "cold" situation, and Frank picked up on it. She would try anything, it seemed, to get him to see things from her point of view.

Frank, on the other hand, saw Sally's absence as an opportunity for him and his daughter to have a little fun. The "ogre" was gone! Out came the cookies, in went the videotape, and father and daughter sat up watching television and eating junk food until 9:00 P.M., when Sally walked in. She found the two of them curled up on the couch. Suddenly the room became very tense.

Funny thing about this encounter. Though both parents acted surprised when they saw each other, they really weren't surprised at all. Deep down inside, Sally knew Frank wouldn't do as she had asked him to do concerning putting Ellen to bed on time. That's why she had mentioned the cold Ellen "seemed" to be coming down with. She would use it later as a weapon to make

Frank feel guilty about keeping Ellen up past her bedtime. Sally came in the door expecting to see what she saw.

Frank also knew his wife would eventually come home and find father and child sitting together watching television way past the 8:00 P.M. "deadline." In ways like these, Sally and Frank consistently "communicated" their unwillingness to compromise.

What transpired that night was a full-blown verbal assault over the fact that Ellen had been allowed to eat cookies, watch TV, and miss her bedtime. Sally screamed that Frank couldn't be trusted to take care of his own child. "Even the fourteenyear-old baby-sitter is more responsible that you!" she accused hotly. Frank blasted her back with the shot that Sally was so "rigid she was frigid!" All these ridiculous statements were being hurled back and forth with little Ellen watching, wide-eyed, from the couch. Things had gotten way out of hand.

The verbal battle was intense that night. When Sally and Frank awoke the next morning, they were both scared. Frank had slept on the couch because he was too proud to come to bed. Each was scared that something had been lost from the marriage. Now both were ready to talk.

"Let's get a baby-sitter and get out of the house tonight," Sally suggested as she handed Frank his morning cup of coffee. He drank it in the kitchen with Sally standing nearby, each spouse refusing to make eye contact. "Better yet," Frank suggested, "let's drop Ellen off at Doreen's and spend the morning out together. I'll call my office and tell them to cancel my appointments." That shocked Sally.

Risk for the Sake of the Relationship

Compromise does not come easy. Until it happens, however, a couple cannot function as one. Sometimes it takes a shock like the one that jolted Sally and Frank for two people to see the big picture. Both Sally and Frank were concerned about the issue at hand—parenting Ellen. Yet the atmosphere they were creating by their lack of compromise was disastrous for the whole family.

Sally and Frank weren't working together to solve the problem of parenting little Ellen. It's not like they were in limbo over the issues. Each of them had been working hard on their parenting techniques . . . against each other! Caught in the middle was Ellen. After a point, the issues didn't seem to matter as much as winning the parental tug of war.

During the squabbles over the Vietnam peace talks, thousands of lives were lost—all because the negotiators could not come to terms over who should sit where at the peace table.

"But it's so hard to give in on this issue," Sally began that morning as she and Frank sat drinking coffee at a nearby diner. "I feel like things such as an established bedtime are of the utmost importance for Ellen's development. She needs to learn to live within a system! It's important for her future."

"We have gotten to the point where she lives for the sake of your stupid system," Frank countered, then added, "I'm sorry . . . I shouldn't have said that. It's just that I'm so frustrated that I feel like I've got to get permission before Ellen and I can have any fun."

"You think I like being the ogre?" Sally asked wearily. "I hate the fact that Ellen's face lights up when she thinks it's you coming through the door. Then her little smile fades when she sees it's only me." With that, Sally burst into tears.

This was a very important morning for Frank and Sally. This was the morning when they came to grips with the fact that they needed to find some common ground . . . for the sake of their marriage. As hard as compromise might seem to each of them, their marriage and Ellen's future suddenly seemed more important than their differing opinions about parenting.

The next step for these two parents was to be willing to listen to each other and accept the other person's ideas, even if they did not agree on every point. Sometimes a spouse's ideas can be so out of line that they are hard to accept. Still, if those ideas are not outside the boundaries of one's belief system, perhaps they're worth a try. As far as our household is concerned, anything that is not outside the boundaries of what Christ or the Bible would have us do is worth the risk. For the sake of marital growth and familial tranquility, Rosemary and I will risk compromise.

Why Are We Here Together?

"Why did you call me frigid?" Sally asked, as if the word *frigid* had struck her in the heart. Frank looked down at the table before responding, "You're not frigid—you're just hard to reach sometimes." He went on to talk to her about her comment that he was sometimes more irresponsible than the couple's fourteen-year-old baby-sitter. He told her that her need for constant control sometimes made him feel like less than a man. He said he sometimes felt like her second child. Sally listened and resisted the impulse to tell him why she felt she needed to treat him like that.

As they talked, Sally and Frank saw what their lack of compromise had been doing to their marriage. They saw how it had been affecting every area of their lives. Even their sex life had been affected by their differing opinions on parenting. Or was it really their differing opinions?

More than their differences, it was the way they had been handling those differences that had created the most problems for Sally and Frank. They had to be willing to compromise and give enough ground to end the war. Sally said, "But what if I totally disagree with the way you handle Ellen's bedtime?"

"Then we will have to weigh the importance of each of the issues in terms of the bigger picture," Frank said. "One of us will have to compromise. I mean, why are we really here? We're here because we love each other, but we're battling over stupid things. It's been making it hard for us to even look at each other, let alone sleep in the same bed."

One thing was certain. If compromise would ever be reached, at least one partner had to be willing to come over to the other partner's side.

Frank demonstrated the importance of such measures both literally and figuratively when he suddenly got up from the table. Ellen gasped. She thought he was walking out on her! Instead, he came around to her side of the table, sat down next to her, and put his arm around her. "Nothing is worth fighting like this," he began. "I won't battle you anymore on these issues!"

At this point, due to Frank's initial leadership, Sally came over to his side on the issues. "I guess you're right. I've been too rigid, just trying to make my point." They were now in compromise mode. Better yet, they were in communication mode.

Compromise Leads to One Flesh

When the Bible refers to "one flesh," it is in reference to two people getting married and becoming one person—not just sexually, but in every way. That is accomplished over a long period of time through various forms of communication. It will never be accomplished unless each spouse is willing to compromise. Compromise must take place in the areas of finance, sexual intimacy, parenting, and every other area of the marital blend—even television watching. If only one spouse is called to submit, the marriage won't blend and become one flesh.

Compromise boils things down to a common standard or goal. As they sat drinking coffee in the diner that morning, Sally and Frank decided to make Christ their common standard by which to make all future marital and parenting decisions. It didn't all come together that day, however. They had to work at using the standards of Christ to bring compromise toward a common good for their home and marriage. As they worked together to compromise, they found their love for each other had grown by leaps and bounds. No longer did one of them have to win. As a result, the *marriage* was winning! They had tried to use the fickle standards of society—the ones that change so quickly according to the latest fads and whims. Now they were trying the consistency of Christ's standards—the One who knew the inner desires of their hearts.

"If Christ were present at this table as we are talking, what would He want us to do?" This phrase became their motto. Over time the motto helped Sally and Frank see what was really important—that winning an argument was not nearly as important as finding a solution that both could live with . . . a solution pleasing to Christ.

Ironically, their compromise toward each other's point of view was the best thing they could have done to help their daughter, Ellen. She now had the opportunity to grow up in a more consistent environment with two parents who didn't fight as often as they once did. None of this would have happened, however, if one of them hadn't decided to come over to the other's side, regardless of the opinions currently being debated. Otherwise each would try to dominate instead of communicate.

Summary

1. Communication requires compromise. Without compromise in a marriage, one person will dominate . . . and no one will communicate.

2. Someone must start the compromise process by coming over to the other person's side of the communication table.

3. Both spouses must look at the bigger picture. Are they losing the war over just one battle?

4. Compromise should take place in every area of marriage to prevent destructive nonverbal signals.

Communication Keys

1. List some of the issues that you and your spouse generally disagree on (finances, sexual issues, parenting, etc.).

2. How do you handle those differences? Is there a better way?

3. What standards do you and your spouse use to help reach compromise on the difficult issues (standards of your parents, culture, or biblical standards, etc.)?

Part 5

HEART-LEVEL COMMUNICATION

20

When Serious Problems Have Warped the Door Closed

So much had happened between the two of them. In the last year, however, it seemed there had been nothing but heartbreak. After eight years of marriage Susan had fallen into a horrible trap. She found herself involved in an extramarital affair. As would be expected, her husband, Tim, was devastated. The couple had gone for counseling and were attempting to put the relationship back together. But they rarely talked to each other anymore.

"How can we talk?" Tim finally blurted out to the counselor one day. "How can I talk to someone I can't even trust?"

Tim and Susan were still living under the same roof, and Susan was no longer involved in that brief affair. In fact, she was very sorry and could not believe that she had been so foolish! She begged Tim to forgive her. Everything seemed to be heading back the way it was before she made her mistake, but there was something missing.

Dottie was dealing with a different situation. For many years her husband, Dave, had been talking as if he was just on the verge of the big deal. These words had so frequently rolled off Dave's lips that to hear them now made Dottie sick to her stomach. "Everything's going to be different . . . soon." What she could really no longer tolerate hearing, however, were the words, "Trust me!"

"Trust me! We're on the verge of the big one!" Dottie's salesman husband would frequently say. But nothing would ever happen. Dave's enthusiasm would die out for a while, then be revived again when he became excited over his work once more. The words "trust me" would start flowing her way again, but nothing seemed to change. They lived a very tight, hand-to-mouth existence.

Dottie wanted to trust her husband. She wanted to believe in him. She certainly wanted things to improve. She had gotten to the point where she was afraid to get her hopes up. Dave seemed like such a ridiculous dreamer. The things he'd promised her when they first got married were now nothing more than distant dreams. Their marriage had reached the place where she couldn't stand the sight of Dave. She planned to stay married to him, but she didn't have to like him. They couldn't communicate about anything without Dottie making razor-sharp comments. Something was missing from this marriage and it wasn't money. It wasn't even the accumulation of all those unfulfilled dreams.

One last story has to do with Cindy, a wife who spent her childhood in a very abusive home. She never got past that trauma, but she had gotten married anyway. Cindy thought marriage would clean the slate and help her start over with relationships. Unfortunately, it didn't work that way. Seven years of marriage later and she was still finding it difficult to relate to her husband, Paul.

Paul was a wonderful man, very gentle and patient. Instead of pouring her life into pleasing Paul, she acted as if she couldn't trust that he would not hurt her as she had been hurt in the past. She was very distant and cold toward him. Cindy even acted like she needed to protect their four-year-old daughter from him, although he had gone out of his way to relieve her of any fears. Cindy didn't want to talk to him about the fears . . . or about anything else, for that matter. Theirs was more of an arrangement than a fulfilling marriage.

Cindy and Paul had a problem on their hands and they couldn't talk about it. Their communication had been totally cut off for reasons that had nothing to do with their marriage relationship.

When You Stop Loving

Each of these marriages was suffering from the same problem. The circumstances were different but the root problem was
basically the same. Each of the marriages had been damaged by
an invasion that had violated the sanctity of the relationship.
For Susan and Tim an extramarital affair had stolen Tim's trust
for his wife from their relationship. For Dottie and Dave, it was
the realization that one of them was a dreamer and the other a
realist that had extinguished the fires of their relationship.
Cindy's marriage was dampened long before she met Paul. Trau-
matic episodes from her childhood had caused her to crawl into
a hole to protect her heart from the possibility of future violation and more pain. She had decided that she would never be
hurt again . . . and Paul was suffering for it.

Each of these marriages is now past the danger zone. Even
Dottie has worked past her difficulties. Deep down inside she
knows her husband will never land the big one, so she no longer
has to deal with that expectation. Each couple or individual has
sailed past his or her own nasty coral reef. They've gotten past the
events that caused the initial pain, yet they continue to live as if
the old problems are still imminent. They still treat their partners
like the potential for shipwreck is dead ahead. Though the circumstances may be different in each of these marriages, in each
one communication has shut down due to lack of forgiveness.

The Greatest Deterrent to Communication

Communication can be devastated by many events. No
event is as damaging as how a couple may respond to it. When
one spouse does not forgive the other, the communication becomes handicapped until forgiveness takes place.

Years ago I taught on a college campus. We used general
classrooms, which meant that I rotated use of a classroom with
several other instructors. In one particular case, the instructor
who had used the room right before me was a major chalkboard
user. He wrote on every single inch of it. When I came into the

classroom the board was always covered with his scribbled notes. The first thing I had to do was spend several minutes erasing the board so I could find some space for my own notes.

One afternoon as I arrived in class, I noticed that someone had borrowed our eraser. Retrieving a paper towel from the restroom, I erased the board the best I could. After class, I was sitting out in the room with a student, discussing his paper, when I casually looked up at the board. It was unreadable. "I can't believe it!" I said to the student. "That board is unreadable! You can't tell which notes are mine and which notes were there from the previous class! Could you guys read my notes?"

"Hardly," the student replied. "You worked so hard trying to erase the board that nobody had the heart to tell you that we still couldn't tell what you were writing on the board."

It's the same with communication in marriage. Things happen that fill up the board. If they are not erased from time to time, future communication can be hampered. Each of these couples had things in their marriages or previous relationships that needed to be erased—things that required forgiving someone else.

Without taking steps to forgive, past emotions bleed through into present relationships and hamper all current and future communication. Forgiveness helps erase the past and its pain. Then the board can be clean once more so couples can communicate and continue to work on their relationship.

Some couples must decide to forgive their spouse for major violations, while others must forgive a series of smaller, daily offenses. Cindy had to forgive someone, but it wasn't her spouse who had hurt her. Even though her husband was on the receiving end of her pain and anger, it was family members of her past that she really needed to forgive. Until she did, there would be no heart-level communication between her and her husband Paul.

Start with a Decision

Decide to forgive—that's the key. Forgiveness is an action one must choose to take. A spouse must decide to forgive the one who offended or hurt him or her.

Forgiveness is not an attitude or action that comes naturally to anyone. No one will wake up one morning and feel like forgiving another person for something he or she said or did. Forgiveness is a choice. Few books have done a better job of describing this process than *Forgive and Love Again* by John Neider and Thomas Thompson. It is "must" reading for every couple.

There are different levels of forgiveness. Each of the couples described in this chapter needed to forgive for different reasons. In each case, forgiveness would begin with a decision. Then it would be possible to move on in the communication and healing processes.

"What if my spouse, or my abusive stepparent, never comes to me and asks to be forgiven?" a person may ask. Forgiveness is not dependent upon waiting for the offending party to ask for forgiveness. If that were the case poor Cindy would be doomed for life. If she couldn't get out from under the burden of her pain until her stepfather came to her and asked for her forgiveness, she would be in trouble. He might never do it. Then how would she ever find the freedom to love and communicate with Paul? Her "blackboard" would never be clean from past filth.

Forgiveness is not dependent on the offender's asking to be forgiven. However, the continuation of a meaningful relationship with the offender may be dependent on his asking for forgiveness. It's difficult to maintain a relationship with a person who refuses to acknowledge the pain he or she has caused. That certainly doesn't mean that person should be controlled by the offender's lack of repentance. To the contrary, the offended person needs to reach down inside herself and choose to forgive the offender regardless of whether there has been any repentance. Whether a meaningful relationship continues after forgiveness has taken place is a whole different issue.

This is obviously easier said than done. Forgiveness is a difficult action to take—an action requiring communication if it is to be successful. It's a step-by-step process, made by choice. It's ironic that communication is a necessary ingredient in order to begin the process of forgiveness. Yet communication will be tremendously hindered if the forgiveness does not take place.

Communication will start the wheels of forgiveness rolling, and forgiveness will help spouses continue to develop meaningful communication in the future. Forgiveness and communication in marriage are interrelated.

Steps Toward Forgiveness

Step 1: *Decide there is no option but to forgive.* The Author of love and forgiveness has written much in the Bible about the action of forgiveness. "Forgive us our sins, just as we have forgiven those who have sinned against us" (Matt. 6:12 TLB). In this section of the Lord's Prayer, it is understood that in order to be forgiven, we must forgive. In fact, we are required to forgive. If we don't, we will not receive forgiveness (v. 15). God knew each of us would need instruction in this area. That's why we memorize the Lord's Prayer, which teaches this most basic concept of human relationships—the concept of forgiveness. We must forgive in order to be healthy. We must forgive so we can have a good marriage. We must forgive so we can communicate with our spouses without any hidden agendas. It's a command from God. God knew we needed to learn to forgive so we could participate in loving another person.

Step 2: *Talk about it.* Communication is a pivotal part of the forgiveness process. That certainly does not mean anyone should continually rehash the failures that led to past pain. Susan should not be forced by her husband, Tim, to talk about the details of the affair. As J. Allen Peterson points out in his classic book, *The Myth of Greener Grass,* talking about the details will only further ingrain the mental videotapes of the affair in both the minds of Susan and Tim. And that will only cause more pain.

Communication should include talking about better times. It should include an openness to talk about all the things Tim does to make Susan feel like she is still guilty. Susan should delicately talk to Tim about the way he continually makes her feel like dirt. Tim needs to hear these difficult things without blowing up, even if he still feels he deserves to be angry. "After all, look what has been done to me!" What he's really thinking or feeling is, "Look what you've done to me, Susan!" That's not choosing to forgive!

Communication that seems so difficult at this point is extremely important. Some couples have found it easier to begin the communication process with the help of a professional counselor or pastor. It must take place, however. Both parties should resist rehashing the sordid details while talking freely of their current feelings.

Step 3: *Forgiveness is a choice, not a feeling.* "But I don't *feel* like forgiving her! The pain is so great and she acts as if it's over and done with . . . but it's not. The affair may be over, but the pain is still there. How can I forgive when I don't feel like it?"

Decide not to be controlled by circumstances. While talking with your spouse, there will be things that will remind you of painful situations. Stop, get control again, and don't let those painful thoughts control you.

Those who don't take action and forgive the one who hurt or offended them will either be controlled by anger or the circumstances that caused the pain. Feelings—especially painful ones—will take control and blur the possibility of all meaningful communication.

Take action and overcome those feelings of pain and anger. It's as if a horrible accident has happened, leaving a person's legs severely damaged. The wounded person must decide not to give up. He must decide to learn to walk again. Although he may not feel like it, and although walking is very painful, he must start walking once more.

Step 4: *Forgive . . . for an hour at a time.* Forgiveness is not necessarily a once-and-for-all decision. One of the most discouraging things to Susan and Tim was the fact that they could have a wonderful time of communication one night . . . and the next morning feel like nothing had happened. Susan would begin to feel as if Tim was getting past his pain and that he had his wife back totally . . . then morning would come. Once again he would hardly look her in the eye, let alone talk to her in a civil manner. It was making both of them crazy.

Forgiveness is like learning to walk again after an accident. Each morning you may need to learn to walk all over again. Each morning you may need to decide to take action . . . again . . . to forgive the one who hurt you. "How long will I have to go through this?" Tim asked his counselor. "Until you can get up and walk," the counselor replied.

Step 5: Know that you, too, have been forgiven of much. I remember once saying that to a very righteous lady. She looked at me as if to say, "Who do you think you're talking to? What do you mean that I should remember that I, too, have been forgiven much?" So often we act as if we have lived very puritanical lives, needing no forgiveness for ourselves. But everyone needs forgiveness. The only perfect One chose to forgive you and me . . . and He offered forgiveness to us by paying a horrible price. God chose to send His Son so each of us may be forgiven. If God chose to forgive you and me, who are we to refuse to forgive those who have offended us?

Are my standards higher than God's? I think not!

Communication Will Be Enhanced by the Forgiveness Process

Not only is communication central to the ongoing forgiveness process, it is also enhanced by it. As forgiveness takes place, marital communication will get better and better. There will no longer be walls of anger and resentment separating the couple. Pain will begin to subside and each spouse will once again be able to risk nakedness in the marriage.

I remember seeing a cowboy movie in which all the men were required to check their guns at the sheriff's office as they rode into town. One of the cowboys talked about how naked he felt without his guns. The sheriff said everyone would be safer if nobody had guns.

Everyone is safer when no one has any weapons to hide behind. When we are all "naked," without weapons or other forms of camouflage to hide behind, then we can talk. When a couple is naked, free from the pain they have caused each other in the past, they can communicate. Then they can feel free to communicate their love at heart level without the risk of getting shot at by their partner.

Communication Can Be a Healing Ointment

Without forgiveness, communication is either at a very surface level—or worse, it can be used as a weapon. In Dottie's case Dave had continually said, "Trust me! The big sale is just around the corner!" His empty promises had caused their communication to become indifferent. Dottie never really listened to anything Dave had to say these days.

In Susan's case, because the affair had raped Tim's trust in her, their communication was like walking through a mine field. Tim waited for Susan to talk as if things were better, then he would explode. He'd quickly remind her of how unfaithful and unworthy she was. He was communicating, "Don't you dare act as if things are back to normal!"

Each of us must communicate to help each other heal. Communication can be a great weapon . . . or it can be a healing salve. The choice is up to each individual.

Lower the Drawbridge

South Florida has many canals. Drawbridges are very popular here. Usually at the most inopportune times, the draw-bridge over one of the canals goes up, stopping traffic for several minutes while boats too tall for the bridge move through its temporary opening. Once a drawbridge near my neighbor-hood became stuck. The drivers had to turn their cars around and forget about using that particular road until the bridge was repaired.

Communicating is like the bridge that links two partners in marriage. The everyday happenings of life can create a draw-bridge that may be pulled up from time to time within the marriage. When that happens, communication stops tempo-rarily and the link in the relationship is broken.

Unforgiveness is one of the things that can cause a marital drawbridge to become stuck in the up position. When there is no forgiveness, the communication flow is shut down. Slowly the two partners become disconnected . . . and eventually each looks for alternate routes to get his or her needs met.

Actual drawbridges are operated by a complex system of hydraulics. When these fail to function, the bridges must be raised and lowered by an old-fashioned lever that is worked by hand. It is not only somewhat dangerous, but also tedious. The operators cannot just sit back and push buttons during these times of hydraulics failure. They must get up, bypass the computer, and work the levers furiously . . . like they did in the good old days.

It's always risky to forgive and begin to move on in a marital relationship. It's risky because you may be hurt again. It may seem easier to abandon the relationship altogether and refuse to communicate or forgive. If you don't forgive, you can't communicate. Anger builds up inside and all communication can be cut off. When you refuse to forgive (and "refuse" is the correct word, since forgiveness is by choice), you will have no relationship. Worse yet, you will have no relationship with the One who created you. "For if you forgive men when they sin against you, your heavenly Father will also forgive you. But if you do not forgive men their sins, your Father will not forgive your sins" (Matt. 6:14, 15 NIV).

It's interesting that the need to forgive is such a vital element of our emotional health. Much more significant, however, it is the biblical mandate from the One who created us. He forgave . . . so we could forgive. Now we *must* forgive!

Summary

1. The lack of forgiveness will destroy the whole communication process.
2. Forgiveness is a choice each person must make.
3. No spouse should hold the other spouse prisoner by refusing to forgive.

4. Choosing to forgive is not only necessary in order to restore communication in a marriage, but it is mandatory for the existence of the relationship.

Communication Keys

1. What are some of the things your spouse has done in the past that you are still angry about?
2. What are some areas where you are having a hard time trusting your spouse due to something that occurred in the past?
3. What are some things you feel your spouse still holds against you?
4. Decide to forgive and release those past emotions so you and your spouse can work on future communication together.

Further Reading on This Topic

Forgive and Love Again, John Neider and Thomas Thompson, Harvest House.

Love Is a Decision, Gary Smalley and John Trent, Word.

21

"Pull, Don't Push, Stupid!"

I felt so ridiculous! I was to be the next speaker on stage at the conference center, but I couldn't get to the stage. I found myself walking down a hallway in a conference center I had never seen before. Carrying all my notes, I came to a door that led up onto the stage. As I leaned into the door, trying to push it open, I couldn't get it to budge. Try as I might, that door—one of those big, heavy, fire-rated doors—was jammed tight. I weigh 190 pounds, but no matter how hard I tried I couldn't get the door open. I put my shoulder into it, trying to bulldoze it open. I couldn't believe it! I was already supposed to be on stage—just on the other side of that door—but someone had obviously locked me out.

In a panic, I gave the door one more push. As I did, I glanced at a small handwritten sign that had been taped to the middle of the door: "Pull, Don't Push, Stupid!" By now, I was nervous enough that I'd try anything to get onto that stage. I felt like a total idiot. I looked around sheepishly to see if anyone had seen me trying to frantically plow through a door that a child could have easily pulled open. Then I pulled it open, trying to act as if I had known how to do it all the time!

I think this is a perfect closing illustration to show how many couples misuse the whole communication process. You probably bought this book, hoping Rosemary and I would tell you how to get your point across to your spouse. You probably thought, "Finally! A book that will help me tell my spouse about my needs!" Both spouses—and in some cases just one spouse—spend the marriage trying to communicate by *pushing* their mates into seeing things their way. When it happens that both

218

spouses are trying to push their own opinions, they often find themselves pushing *against* each other.

Like that door leading to the stage that I had pushed so hard to open, the door to each other's heart becomes jammed shut. When two people are pushing from opposite sides, the door of communication won't budge. When just one person continually pushes his or her opinions or agendas, the same problem can occur. The other spouse winds up locking the door because it is less tiresome to just close off listening and lock himself or herself behind that door than to fight the issue. These spouses hear some noise, but they no longer hear what their partner is actually saying.

Marital Communication Can't Be Pushy

Imagine a person trying to push a door open that should be pulled open! It conjures up an image of me trying to open that fire-rated door. That's how we're taught to communicate in today's world. Learn to talk so people will listen! Learn to talk so people won't take advantage of you! Be assertive! Get your way! Take control! These and a host of other phrases sum up what this generation has been taught in terms of how to aggressively speak our minds. That pushy attitude may make a person successful in the business world. However, it will most assuredly make one lonely in a marriage.

Marriage was intended to be a blending of two people. It is difficult for two people to blend into one beautifully functioning couple when one spouse is attempting to dominate the relationship. There's a big difference between two blending and one dominating. Communication is the vehicle that will help a couple blend and become more like one. Two people can't blend when both are lined up on opposite sides of the door, pushing for all they're worth. They just push the door closed even more tightly. No blend of two hearts takes place when the door of communication is slammed tight between them. Worse yet, neither partner will find the happiness made possible by the blending of two people into one couple.

Why Not Push?

I had to pull on that door leading to the stage in order to get it open. The action of pulling is very different from pushing. When you push on a door to open it, you barely have to break stride. You just put your shoulder into it . . . and everyone on the other side had better get out of the way! The door flies open and you keep right on plowing straight ahead in the same direction.

Pulling, on the other hand, means you have to stop and make room for the door to open toward you. It's a much more humbling action than pushing. The door doesn't fly open as easily. Instead, you must move out of its path as it swings toward you.

This is how couples should respond to one another. Both spouses should be willing to get out of the way and draw the other person toward them. Listen . . . don't just plow right on through!

Today's couples usually approach marriage with both partners pushing for their needs to be met. People marry, push open their emptiness, and immediately start demanding, "Fill it! It's empty!" In other words, each is saying, "Meet my needs! Meet my needs!" Instead of coming into the marriage with a willingness to give, today's couples come expecting to instantly receive. Instead of coming into a marriage to learn about the other partner, today's couples come to the marriage telling the other person what they want. Many of today's individuals come to the marriage for the purpose of talking instead of listening.

In a previous chapter, we referred to the book, *The Secret Garden*. When its heroine finally finds her way through the hidden door in an ivy-covered wall, she finds the vegetation in the garden in horrible disarray. She could have looked at it and walked away. She could have plowed everything under. Instead, she saw potential for a beautiful garden there. She carefully tended it and nursed it back to health. She chose to put forth an effort for the sake of the garden and spent many hours each day painstakingly nurturing and coaxing the plants back to flourishing good health. She was exuberant over the tiniest bit of progress. The smallest green shoot received her loving toil and care.

Once the heroine in *The Secret Garden* had responded to the needs of the untamed, unloved plot of ground behind the ivy-covered wall, the garden began to bloom. All her work to meet the garden's "needs" began to bear glorious fruit, and she was soon the recipient of its heady mixture of sweet fragrances and lovely, colorful blossoms. That would not have been possible, however, had she not put aside her own needs for the sake of tending to the garden. In the end, experiencing the sights and smells of the beautiful garden brought her great personal joy.

This is what we should do in our marriages. Instead of assertively demanding our rights, we should pull back and allow—even encourage—our spouses to open up and share the contents of their own hearts. We must encourage them to share the expressions on their faces. We must encourage them to share their words. Learning to listen is the real key to every aspect of the marital communication process. Listening allows two people to risk sharing at a level that will continually draw them together more intimately.

A Simple Story

I grew up in a home not very different from the others I knew. Times of trauma helped make me into the tightly closed person I used to be. In my midteens my mother died of cancer and I made an unconscious decision. I determined to close the door to my heart. After the loss of my mom, it seemed safer to lock myself away and never share again. At least I'd never risk getting hurt again! I put a wall around my "garden" to keep everyone out.

Rosemary and I dated for five years before getting married. While we were dating I began to learn how to talk. I found that it was something she wanted to do and something that drew us closer together. It drew me closer to the "prize" of getting her to marry me. I never really opened the gate to the inner me, but I was willing to talk.

In 1972 we were married and almost immediately I found it unnecessary to devote the same amount of time and attention

to communication. It was getting too scary, trying to share
who I really was inside. After all, I wasn't even sure I knew who
I was anymore. Now that we were married, why should I keep
chasing after the prize by spending all that time talking? It was
too risky. The more I opened myself up to my new wife, the
more I risked rejection and pain . . . or so I thought. It just
seemed easier to pursue my own needs by watching lots of television or playing racquetball.

Rosemary had to make a choice during those early years of
our marriage. She had to decide whether or not to try to bulldoze open the door to my heart. She could have easily done it
by demanding that I listen to her needs. The other option was to
read the "sign" instructing her to pull, not push. She decided
to step back and slowly pull on the door to my heart until it
gently opened.

It took about eight years . . . eight years of Rosemary's
taking advantage of every opportunity to listen to me during
the infrequent times when I would open up. During those times
she was often tempted to say, "Is it my turn? Can I talk about my
needs now?" She rarely did that, however. By listening with an
earnestness that made me feel like I had something important
to say, Rosemary encouraged me to keep right on opening up.

As she gently pulled instead of forcibly pushing, I learned
how to risk sharing the inner me. Her listening also taught me how
to listen to her. I had never had to listen to anyone before. I had
never even seen it done. Prior to marriage, I had come to believe
that a person had to take what he could get from life and guard
himself from having to give anything back. After eight years of
marriage, I slowly began to realize that I had kept the door to my
inner self locked for too long. I kept myself locked away because
I was afraid that if people got to know the real me, they would
think me pathetically shallow and weak.

Slowly Rosemary pulled the door open, all the while posi-
tioning herself out of the way. Slowly I risked . . . until we were
each able to open the doors of communication and experience a
level of relationship that truly caused us to work toward becoming one flesh.

It's Humbling!

Pulling can be a very humbling posture. It means having to get out of the way. When people see the big picture so well that they don't mind humbling themselves for the sake of the relationship, it can mean an opportunity to follow the example of the heavenly Bridegroom.

The great Bridegroom, after sitting on the throne of heaven, saw the tremendous need of His bride. Continually the Bible portrays Christ as the Bridegroom and the church as His bride. The picture we see is of the King, Jesus Christ, seated on His throne in heaven with all privileges and power. Upon "hearing" the needs of His bride, the Bridegroom put aside His own needs to come down from heaven and begin life on earth as a baby, born into the most humble of circumstances . . . a stable. Eventually He would choose to die for the sins of mankind. He sacrificed Himself for the needs of His bride. If that's not a picture of humility, then a picture doesn't exist.

The picture is for us. Communication is so vital! It is designed to help us better understand the needs of our spouse, not put there so we can "push" to get our own needs met. We must pull together, not push each other away.

Don't Forget to Read the Instructions!

Reading the instructions would have kept me from ruining the key-card at the hotel in the episode I related earlier in the book. It was humbling for me to go back to that pleasant clerk and ask for help to get my hotel room door open. I was embarrassed to tell her that I had broken the key-card off in the lock. Secretly I knew that if I had just taken the time to read the instructions, I might have already had the door open and been snoring by then. But I thought that little plastic card would be a cinch for someone as intelligent as me to operate!

The key to using one of those cards, it seems, is to take your time. Don't get in a hurry. Don't just jam it in the slot. If I had first read the directions the key manufacturers had conveniently placed above each slot, I would have had great results. When I did that—presto!—the door opened wide.

I learned how to successfully operate one of those plastic keys by the mistakes I made that night. Once I had read the directions, I had the hang of it after just a few tries. Now hotel doors across the country swing wide open for me because I know how to operate the key.

Marriage is a lot like that. The Maker of marriage has given us an instruction manual—the Bible. If we take time to read the directions, then—presto! . . . well, maybe not presto . . . we stand a good chance of improving our communication with our spouses. Our marriages can't help but benefit. Reading the instructions, prayerfully seeking God's direction, listening to His response, then listening to our spouses—now that's communication . . . communication at its best.